The LiterART Greyhound

2015

Writing & Art by Johnston Greyhounds

Edited by Cindy Dinneen, Mark Dostert,
Rebecca Mitchell, and Ches Smith

GREYHOUND
PRESS

TABLE OF CONTENTS

ACKNOWLEDGEMENTS

The LiterART Greyhound editorial team would like to thank all the wonderful faculty and staff metmbers at Johnston Middle School. Each and every one of you plays an integral part in the education of our students: Melissa Abercia-Simmons, Courtney Adams, Alexia Adderley, Renikki Alexander, Lisa Arledge, Vinne Arlt, Tobi Arsham, Kristen Aust, William Aust, Elizabeth Bandercan, Deric Barber, Amanda Bates, Derilia Beaubrun, Lanena Berry, Donna Bolden, Chandel Bonner-Hancock, Jo Braxton-Trimble, Todd Brewer, Susan Calvin, Beatriz Canavati, Vasti Cantu, Juan Cao, Dora Carabajal, Jason Carmichael, Edna Carmona, Anna Carrion, Cleonides Chester, Lisa Chilivetis-Turner, Susan Cole, Laurie Conner, Celeste Cooper, Brittney Cornelius-Chapple, Dominic Cowan, Vanessa Curry, Wilfred Dacus, Sonya Davis, Jerri De Leon, Andrew DeWalt, Talton Edmond, Regina Ellis, Jaclyn Figurski, Jason Flores, Mary Ford, Darrell Fortin, Yumi Franklin, Peggy French, James Fry, Matthew Garner, Margaret Given, Danyetta Godwin, Janet Gray, John Green, Caryn Grimm, Diane Grosscope, Benjamin Grube, Roberto Guinea, Christina Gonzalez, Peggy Haehl, Tristan Hardeman, Jasmine Harris, Bruce Hartman, Latricia Hatton-Hunter, Joyce Helfman, Margaret Hines, William Hoffman, Meliza Hull-Frederick, Sherita Jackson, Claran Johnson, Kelli Johnson, Chelsea Kennedy, John Latchett, Traci Latson, Tanisha Lee, Gary Leger, Mitzi Levine, Gina Lingo, Tiffany Lopez, Susana Loredo, Editha Manalese, Don Marion, Alexis Marks, Lucia Martinez, Monique Mason-Kelly, Carl Matherly, Stephen Mathis, Patricia May, Renda McFarland, Rolethial McKelvey, Karen Bartlett, Stephanie Miller, Erin Mione, Rachel Nash, Valerie Novy, Gira Patel, Chadwick Peters, Lisa Pierson, John Quinn, Elesia Reed, Marianne Ritchie, Michael Rivera, Hubert Roberson, Margarita Robles, Jose Rocha, Ana Rodriguez, Fernando Rodriguez, Gail Ross, Chastity Rubin, Kellee Sanchez, Wenden Sanders, Yvette Schultz, Cederick Scott, Leticia

Sendejas, Gregory Siegrist, Johnny Simmons, Lisa Smith, Rose Solodyna, Joseph Sooter, Lucara Stewart, Carla Stutts, Marian Thomas, Sarah Thornburgh, Berta Torano, Lydie Tran, Maria Turner, Sara Vershier, Jennifer Wood, Patricia Wood, Talina Woodard, William Wright, Jason Wyatt, Clara Yates.

You are all *greatly* appreciated!

FOREWORD

"All art is a form of imitation." So says the nineteenth-century Russian writer, Leo Tolstoy. And he certainly was one to talk, he the author of the 1,100-page novel, *War and Peace*, as well as the 225-word flash fiction gem, "The Old Grandfather and His Little Grandson." So exactly what 'art is imitated' in a telephone book-sized narrative of your country's revolution and battlefield encounters with Napoleon? Likewise what 'art' could prompt a razor-sharp, intimate, and yet ironic domestic anecdote revealing how children adapt the behavior and attitude of the adults around them? I suspect that this 'art,' the 'art' this titan of world literature speaks of, might simply be life itself. Tolstoy's life included revolution's instability and death as well as quiet, poignant moments between family members--the ones we never forget, just like we never forget war and death and revolt. So Tolstoy knew peace. He knew war. And he figured out that both could be art. Reading and viewing these students' submissions, I admired our so very young writers and artists doing what Tolstoy did--converting all of life (its peace and its war) into art, be it visual or written, be it images or words in all their possible glorious arrangements. Both merit our contemplation. I confess my jealousy at such advanced aesthetic sensibilities. Oh to be so young and so perceptive! They're seeing and understanding and illustrating right now what I didn't until my late 20s when my first publication appeared. These 'students' are ahead of me, ahead of many of us, in their ability to point us to life and the art in life, albeit in certain moments as full of sadness and confusion as joy and beauty. Such is life and such should be art. It would serve us well to look and listen!

Mark Dostert
7th Grade English Teacher
Author of *Up in Here: Jailing Kids on Chicago's Other Side*

EDITOR'S PREFACE

Did you know that Jane Austen and Agatha Christie struggled mightily with spelling and grammar? That Ernest Hemingway had trouble with present participles? A biographer for William Butler Yeats said, "Yeats' spelling, indeed, seems at times a matter of wildly errant guesswork." Did you know the original draft of *The Great Gatsby* was chock-full of spelling errors and that its author, F. Scott Fitzgerald, couldn't even spell his friend Ernest Hemingway's last name (he spelled it Hemmingway)?

Johnston Middle School's sixth, seventh, and eighth graders are in *very* good company!

Editing is an essential part of the writing process. When approaching this inaugural edition of *The LiterART Greyhound*, we strived to maintain a balance between preserving the voice and intent of each student while making sure each piece was easy to read and understand. Sometimes that meant inserting commas here and there, breaking up long paragraphs into shorter ones, deleting repetitive words and phrases, or replacing "he" and "she" with personal names (and vice versa). What we *didn't* do, was demand the pieces be rewritten with advanced literary techniques we don't even expect students of this age to know! In many cases, the students themselves provided edits, working alongside their English teachers and our Librarian, Cindy Dinneen, and we made every effort to at least make them aware of changes we made to the final product so they weren't caught unaware.

As for the art, due to the production constraints of the book, we had to limit it to black and white pieces or color pieces that could translate into black and white without drastic diminishment. We strived to maintain the pencil strokes and shading techniques unique to each artist while removing wrinkles and blemishes that are so common for students who tote their masterpieces in binders that look like they've been mauled by wild dogs.

A Collection of Writing and Art

What we hope we've produced here is a creative collection of work that encapsulates the wonder, heartbreak, joy, and struggle of kids in this most awkward of ages. We didn't give them any parameters, they were free to submit anything they wanted, so the end result is an eclectic mix of fiction, poetry, persuasive essays, art, and everything in between.

We hope you enjoy reading it as much as we enjoyed compiling (and editing) it!

Ches Smith
Campus Network Specialist
Author of *Under the Suns*

The LiterART Greyhound

Grafitti Rain
Nadine Abazie, age 12

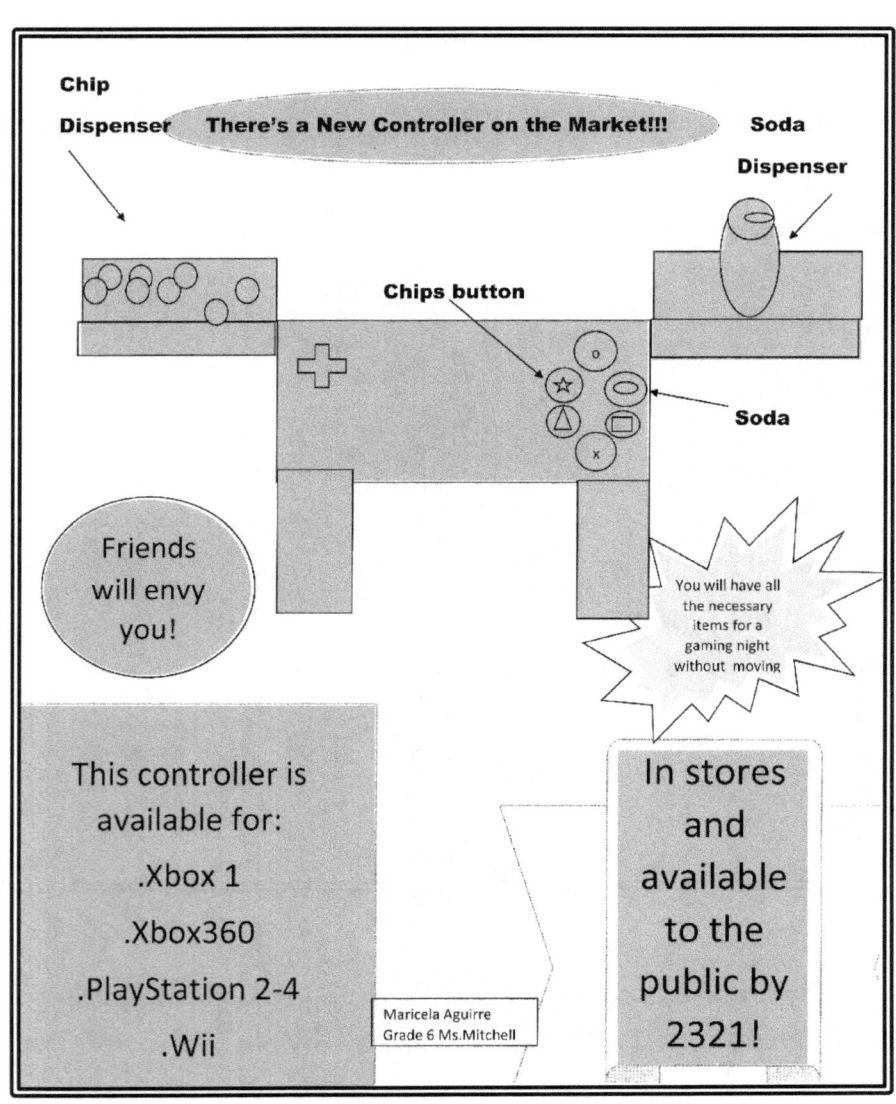

The Coolest Controller
Marciela Aguierre, age 12

Puzzle, Wading, Broken, Wanderers
Ruth Beaubrun, age 14

♦ Puzzle ♦

You treat me like a toy

Sharing me throughout the week

Saying who gets her when

At least

In the past you

Passed me around whole

Now you hold both of my arms

Tearing me

Not in two

Three

Four

Five

Gradually

Making me so weak

Silencing me before I speak

I don't get to yell

I don't get to scream

Even though it's not my fault

You still won't give me a chance to

Sing

My problems

Yell my pain

You'll say I'm complaining

That seems to be

The only thing you two

Can agree to

I feel like a pressurized bottle

Defying all the gas laws

As the pressure goes up

My volume stays constant

Denying me a larger place

To spread what I hold

My pieces get smaller

My strength wavers

Causing me to put faith in pebbles

Avoiding the big rocks

'Cause if the big rocks sinks

My trust sinks

My patience and selflessness

hit 'rock' bottom

My anger floats

The pressure rises

My bottle is obliterated

My pieces scatter

Making it harder for the future

To find glue

♦ Wading ♦

I am

Wading

Drowning

In a body

Of my own

Tears and Fears

I am Waiting

Searching

Reaching

For a lighthouse

That just might

Be near

♦ Half Full ♦

The walls of my throat ache

The air grows thick and hot

My body shakes

My skin crawls

My heart grows heavy

My eyes water

My chest shatters

The pieces stabbing into my intestines

The pain intensifies

Sending me into a lake of salt water

The taste is bitter on my tongue

But even as

My body trembles violently

And my hope is swallowed

Into darkness

And my happiness

Deflates

I feel your presence

Your hand knocking on the door

Your comfort

Muffled through the smoke

Your healing

Peeking through

Like the sunlight through my curtains

Momentarily

Through my despair

You reach your hand

Down

To lift me

Up

Drying my tears

Pulling me through

Caressing what is left

Fighting my own will

To get to a place

I want to lock away

But you

Keep me open

Carefully picking the pieces up

Helping me

Store them away

From those

Who stole them away

I may be naïve

But maybe

You are my type

◆ **Wanderer** ◆

I am not a wanderer anymore

I do not linger on

Times two hands

I do not sit in wait

For the future's next hand

I do not curl up alone

And ignore life's threats

I do not lock my heart

Away from my mind

I do not lie in wait

For night's beginning

And morning's end

I am not a wanderer anymore

I live in the present

Relishing its gifts

I open my arms

To those careful with my heart

I seek life's unknown

I dwell in the arms

Of adoration

I shed open tears

Knowing there are eyes

Shedding ones identity

I fill the edges of my heart

Expanding its boundaries

Filling my soul

Resulting in a smile

I let my vocal chords

Vibrate with laughter

Its cause...

I do not know

I do know

I am not a wanderer

Anymore

Aaliyah
Shania Benjamin, age 12

Is Race an Aspect of Culture?
Ella Bernstein, age 13

Is race an aspect of culture? That question alone is the subject of much dispute. Everybody has a different answer. My answer is that no, race is not an aspect of culture. Culture is how you act within a community, while race is just what you look like. You don't have to look like people in a community to be part of it. We are all different, after all. That doesn't mean that we cannot be included in a community if we choose.

Cultures are choices made by groups of humans that have become a way of life for some people. They are the traditions and guidelines that different people choose to follow. Meanwhile, race is a physical characteristic often used to describe somebody's background. Race is not a tradition, whereas traditions are precisely what cultures are made of. Another way of putting it is that we are all born with a certain race. Again, race is a physical characteristic that is with us for all our lives. Culture, however, has to be taught to us. We can't be born with culture, at least not physically. For example, if wearing jeans is a part of American culture, a baby wouldn't be born wearing a pair of Levi's. Simplified, culture is a way of life that we learn as we grow: guidelines of the clothes we wear, the songs we sing, the food we cook. Race is just what we look like. How we look does not limit what we can do.

Do you know an African-American person who does not look or act like the people you've learned about who live in Africa? That's right. They have changed their culture but still have the same skin color as their ancestors who emigrated from Africa. Therefore, we have proof that culture is changeable, whereas race is only alterable depending on your environmental surroundings. Look around you and you will see that there is more proof probably sitting right next to you. You could be looking at somebody whose ancestors had come from Mexico or Central America years and years ago, or they could have just moved here a few years after they were born. You could be looking at someone who came from an Asian or European country. Some people choose to keep ties to their roots through culture, but they have probably altered their culture in one way or another. They probably celebrate the Fourth of July or President's Day, whereas they probably wouldn't have in the place where their ancestors were from. In other words, you have choices when it comes to culture. Race is not a choice that you can make. It's with you for all your life.

Now you can see why race is not an aspect of culture. Race is just a word used to describe your skin color. Culture is how you behave, where you belong. And where you belong should never, ever be dictated by the color of your skin.

Under the Tree
Sydney Bertrand, age 12

Everyone is sleeping.

The year is almost over.

Santa Claus is sneaking,

When children are under their covers.

All the presents are under the tree.

Then the old man goes.

When I wake up to see,

My favorite thing, a rose.

The War & Peace Child
Myles Brown, age 11

THE WORLD SHALL SPLIT IN TWO
A SIDE OF PEACE
A SIDE OF WAR
BATTLING FOR THEIR HOPES FOR
THE WORLD
THE PEACE HAS GOOD HOPES
THE WAR HAS EVIL HOPES
WHEN WAR SEEMS TO BE THE WINNING SIDE
FOR THEN
THE PEACE'S HERO SHALL RISE
AND HAVE A CHOICE
TO LIVE FOR EVIL
OR DIE FOR GOOD

This part of the prophecy has been in my head ever since I was old enough to read. My name is Jackson Blacksmith, one of the few African-American warriors of the peace. It's almost the end of December of 2099. I'm 15 years old, turning 16. There has been unrest between War and Peace for 50 years. War wants to take over the world and use the world's resources to take over more worlds. The Peace side was created to keep them from reaching their goal. And we've done exactly that over the years. Horror ran rampant through the houses of the Peace towns and death visited. It's basically WWIII, except that the whole western hemisphere isn't the good side, everyone that wanted peace moved to the eastern hemisphere. It seemed like the Peace had no hope; none at all.

That's when I came in. My parents were the ones who told me about my life's destiny of being the hero of the world, and who I really am. I am mixed with War and Peace. Then they told me how they met. My mom was living in the Peace village, and my dad was on his way to attack the village. My dad and nine other men were instructed to destroy my mother's village. Once they got there, all immediately attacked, except my dad.

He told me that he hesitated for that moment and realized what he was about to do, which was kill children, mothers, fathers, and even animals just like his team. He realized it was wrong to kill people just to gain power. So he turned on his teammates and battled them all. They did not go down easy, and my dad had lots of cuts, bruises, and wounds from guns, knives, and swords. But he killed all of them with only his hammer like Zeus the Greek god.

After the battle, he felt dizzy and collapsed to the ground. Villagers were heading towards him, and my mom was one of them. They immediately started to heal him with their medicines and foods. After my dad got better, he and my mom spent more time together, and then he decided to change sides and work undercover for the Peace. Eventually, my parents got married and later had me. From then on, my mom taught me things to do in the mind and my dad taught me things to do on the battlefield.

Today is Choosing Day for the new warriors of the Peace, including me. Choosing Day is basically when young men and young women become warriors and choose their gear. I received protective wear for my back, chest, belly, and my whole lower body. Next, I chose wrist armor with unlimited firepower, medicines, and more.

All of a sudden, *BOOM... BANG ...BOOM!*

We were under attack! I quickly took cover to see where my mom was. Once I saw her, I raced her to safety. After that, I grabbed weapons and prepared for the battle. Horror all around me, blood flinging everywhere, bodies of the young falling... Then I saw the general of this attack holding my beat up looking father like a dog.

After that, I was unstoppable. I was killing and saving warriors on the battlefield. At least a thousand warriors were on the field, and I killed about 200 warriors of the War side. I felt like James Bond, Bruce Lee, and a Halo 4 Spartan combined. I went for the general holding my father hostage. The general and I went at it with all our might. After a fierce battle, the general succumbed and I let him go with a warning.

He retreated along with his soldiers to the War side.

If they come back, I will fight to the end. Even if they have a bigger army, I will fight until I am the last warrior—sword, knife, bullet, minute, and second.

Until my last breath, I will fight.

I will fight for Peace.

A Better Tomorrow
L. Burgher, age 13

Seven.

You're staying on the side of the playground where the lower class goes, just like the higher classed told you too. Don't want any trouble, your mom says.

Mom says you're special. You think being special is good, but Mom tells you the Highs don't like special. They'll kill you, she says.

You don't understand why you have to, but you keep quiet.

There's someone walking towards you now. He's high class; you can tell by how expensive his clothes look, and how light his skin is compared to yours. He's gonna beat you up. You move to get out of his way, but he stops you.

He asks your name.

Kaleb, you say. You try to hide the way you're trembling.

His name is Gerard. He says he wants to be friends.

But I'm a low, you say.

He just... laughs.

Gerard doesn't care.

He could be teasing you. This could be some cruel trick. You've heard the horror stories, the tales told to low children to keep them in their place.

But his eyes with their vibrant color normal for highs, they sparkle with such sincerity.

You trust those eyes.

Eight.

Today Gerard took you to the Higher class playground. It's because he can push you higher on the better quality swings, he says. Mom will be mad. But Gerard smiles wide when you reluctantly agree to go with him. You want to see that smile again, you think.

You were both smiling until one of the High parents noticed you; your clothes, the color of your skin. They shout at you and wave their hands, shooing you away from their kids. They insulted you- told you that you had diseases. You're really scared now...

You don't smile at Gerard anymore.

Ten.

Gerard is still your friend... somehow. Mom doesn't trust him. She says he's trying to take advantage of you. You worry about that, too, sometimes. What if he finds out you're... special? You want to trust him. But there are some secrets you must keep, even from him.

It hurts you on the inside to keep things from Gerard, but you nod and say, "Yes Ma'am," when Mom explains that it's for your safety.

You don't tell her you feel safest when you're around him.

Twelve.

Gerard is at your house hanging out with you when you see the T.V. broadcast. Some people in the government are saying that lows are below citizenship. You watch with wide, scared eyes. You don't know much about politics, but you know what that means. When the program is over, you look over towards Mom. She buries her face in the laundry she was folding. Her shoulders were shaking; you think she was crying.

Gerard takes your hand and pulls you into your bedroom, where he holds you while you cry, too.

Thirteen.

A week before your fourteenth birthday is when the report comes in with the Sunday newspaper. You see it before Mom does. It says at the top in big, bold letters, "MUTANT DISCOVERED IN THE SOUTH AND EXECUTED- OFFICIALS HUNTING FOR

MORE." You only manage to read half the article before Mom snatches it away from you, but you did see the picture of a woman with dark skin, completely lifeless. Next to that picture was a photograph of what looked like blood; the normal, human red, but you could see lighter flecks that caught the flash of the camera more than the rest of the thick liquid.

You stand there, watching Mom's face go from a look of concern to horror as she reads the article. The paper falls out of her shaking hands, and she turns and hugs you tight.

You return the embrace. You don't want to let go.

Fourteen.

Segregation laws are in place now; even more so than before. You have to wear Gerard's jacket whenever you're with him to look like a High. But, just to be safe, you two don't go out in public anyway.

But, one afternoon, you and Gerard decided to head out to a nearby bakery. He pays for everything and you stay quiet and close to his side, never drawing attention to yourself.

As soon as you see that the front door to your small home is wide open upon your return, you know something is terribly wrong. You rush inside, fearing for the safety of your mother, and you were right to be afraid.

You find Mom against the wall, he hands being held behind her back by a member of the royal guard. They shout questions at her, asking her where the mutant is. The realization that they're talking about you makes something in your stomach drop.

One of them whips around at the sound of your entrance, takes one look at you, and then lunges forward to grab your wrist. You cry out as you feel a sharp pain rip through your forearm, and you look down to see that he had sliced into your wrist with a small blade. You watch, paralyzed in fear, as dark red blood trickles out, flecked by droplets of bronze. This is what makes you special; this is what has wreaked paranoid-filled havoc on your life.

For a moment, it's like time slows down, and you have a chance to reflect on everything; all the choices you've made, the paths you have taken. You'll probably die, now. Once Gerard sees the reason for you being labeled a mutant, he'll be disgusted. You are a sickness; a genetic glitch in the bloodline. You must be erased in the name of purity. You had a nice life, you guess- wait, what?

You feel yourself being pushed against a wall, and when you open your eyes, you see the guard on the ground, a red mark forming on the side of his face where Gerard had struck him. Your friend then moved to come to your mother's aid, but she screamed for you to leave her, to run away.

You can't move, you can't scream; your body refuses to cooperate. But you are dragged out of the house by Gerard, who scoops you up in his arms easily, being over a foot taller than you, and sprints away on his long, athletic legs.

You bounce along in his grip with each step. You want to run on your own two feet, you think. You want to move; to not burden Gerard with your weight. But you can't move. Your entire body is screaming for your house, your home, for the place you grew up, for the woman who raised and loved you. Go back for her, your heart shouts at you. Save your mom.

Three gunshots are heard from your house, then silence.

You never see Mom again.

Fifteen.

You still have nightmares about that day.

Gerard lives with you now, wherever it is that you live. You don't think you could ever thank him enough. He abandoned his high class life for you. He deemed himself a criminal for you.

You can't fathom why. Quite often do you tell him that he should leave you, but he just smiles wearily and plants his lips against your forehead.

You don't know why he does that. All you know is that whenever he touches you, it makes a sense of warmth spread through your body that you've never felt before, even on the coldest nights. You hope he feels that way, too.

Fifteen and a Half.

Things made a turn for the worse in what seemed like the blink of an eye.

All homes owned by lows have been repossessed or burned. All lows live in special communes now, packed together where the high class can keep an eye on them. Anyone who rebels against High authority is executed immediately.

When you first heard about it, you could hardly breathe, let alone move. Gerard held you until you could speak, and even after you told him countless times that you were fine, he still wouldn't let go.

Sixteen.

There are others like you, you've found out. Lows that rebelled and managed to avoid execution. You've decided that you're safer in numbers, so you've formed a little group. You're the only mutant, but the others look up to you as some sort of leader because of it.

They didn't trust Gerard initially, but after they witness how protective he is over you, they seem to warm up to him. You're glad for that. If Gerard was taken away from you....

You'd rather not think about that.

The others have been talking about fighting back, about forming some sort of resistance. You think it's a good idea in theory. But you don't want more people to die like Mom did. However, they expect you to be the leader of this resistance, since you're the only mutant. You don't want to; You don't want to die. But you quietly nod.

You think you'll try to go about this in a non-violent way, since you have the authority. Gerard says he's proud of you. The comment makes you blush, but you hide it by looking away. He probably still saw it, if his grin is anything to go by.

Seventeen.

Your group has gotten bigger. Now, there are around 20 of you, and through your combined efforts you have established some sort of base camp in a small valley. It's not much, but it's out of the chilling wind's reach and well-camouflaged. There are a few covered places where everyone huddles when it rains. Your 'room' is a small space you and Gerard dug out of the side of the valley. It took a while, and Gerard has to crouch since it was made for your height, but it's yours, and everyone respects your personal space.

Gerard told you that he would sleep where everyone else sleeps, but you didn't let him; you can't sleep by yourself. Your dreams are haunted with constant nightmares and flash backs, but when you're sleeping in Gerard's arms he seems to ward your sleep demons away. What are friends for, right? That's all he is. A friend.

You tell yourself that as you wake up from a dream of Gerard holding your hand and kissing you softly under a willow tree with the glowing sunset warming your back.

You've just been informed that the family of one of your comrades will be executed tomorrow; their parents and very young sister. You immediately push all fears away and make a plan to rescue them. You will not let the Highs shatter someone else's family like they shattered yours.

You leave at dusk.

You don't think you have ever been more scared than you were when you snuck into that compound. It isn't a vacation resort; it's a run-down, cramped lot resembling town homes squashed together, all contained by a brick wall topped with barbed wire. A single metal gate is the only entrance, and it's locked. Even so, you pull your dark hood over your head and let Gerard boost you up to climb over. You pretend not to be ashamed of your physical abilities- or lack thereof- as he scales the gate easily once he helps everyone over. One person remains outside to keep watch as the rest of your small group enters one of the "homes" that is separated from the rest. Inside you find a family, huddled together for warmth as they try to sleep through the night. You gently shake the father to consciousness, and he in turn wakes his family.

It was definitely harder sneaking back out, considering the family was very underfed and weak, but you managed to get them safely back to camp.

You look at the people you just rescued, and the reunion of a family separated by law, and you smile. Maybe you can do this after all.

Eighteen.

Since that time, you have taken part in various rescue missions, and participated in sabotage of the government's communication systems; spray painting over billboards, short-circuiting radio transmissions, and other extremely illegal activities. There's a wanted poster with your face on it posted on almost every street corner. The bounty is high, but you try not to worry. They haven't caught you... yet.

You still deny any and all romantic feelings you may have for Gerard. You don't want to, but it's what's best. He deserves much better than you. You're a sickness, and you would just put him in danger.

Yet, one sleepless night, you and him are laying in your make-shift bed and talking. You speak of better, easier times, when you were kids and weren't on the run from the authorities. You ask him about why he first approached you, all those years ago. He chuckled softly and tells you that you were the prettiest boy he had ever seen, and he wanted to see you smile. You blush profusely and insist that he's lying.

You can hardly hear him when he looks at you and softly asks if it looks like he's lying. Your mutated blood is roaring in your ears.

He's leaning in. Oh dear. What is he doing? His hand reaches up and cups your cheek. This is happening. You can feel his hot breath on your lips. You're so close, so close...

His lips mold against yours. They're soft, even though they're slightly chapped. You bet your lips aren't in that great of shape, taking into account all the hours you have spent worrying away at them with your teeth. You mentally ask yourself if this is wrong. Everyone says it is, that it isn't natural. It feels so natural to you, like in this moment is where you're meant to be.

He pulls back and gazes into your eyes, and you see fear flash across his own. He asks if he had done something wrong.

Your brain had become unresponsive. You simply listen to the warm feeling in your chest and press your mouths together again, this time letting your eyes flutter closed and wrapping an arm around his neck. He sighs in relief against you.

The kiss was sweet, gentle, finally releasing the feelings you both have held back for so long. When he pulls away again he brushes his thumb across your cheekbone and smiles.

I love you Kaleb, he says quietly.

You tell him you love him, too, without any hesitation.

You fall asleep with his arms wrapped around you and your nose buried in his chest.

You can do this. You and Gerard can be the example, that your class doesn't dictate who you are. You can walk hand in hand with him, and lead the world to a better tomorrow.

Nothing
Katie Butler, age 12

As I sit here, indecisive, I try to think. I can't. My English teacher said we had to crank out a story in two weeks and I thought, "This is going to be a piece of cake!" But now, I don't have the foggiest idea what I should write about! I wonder, could I write about my backpacking trip last weekend? Nah, it would just bring back bad memories of that tick... never mind. Oh, I know! How about when I skied for the first time in Michigan? Ugh, no! Get a clue, Katie! It never snows in Texas, much less Houston! What to write, what to write? I can't think of anything! Usually, words come to mind in a snap, but now it feels like my mind is void of everything! It's like a giant vacuum has invaded my mind and sucked all the thoughts out. I literally have no idea what to write.

Ideas. What makes an idea an idea? Well, yes, I know that an idea is a thought that someone hopes to make a reality, but how do you know if you have an idea? Is an idea a simple thought, or a fleeting notion that visits you every once in a while? What if the idea grows so strong that it becomes a figurative actuality inside one's head? Is that why people stare into space or drum their fingers unconsciously? They could be trying to escape to that figurative actuality. Some people have so many ideas that they can't help but stare into space all too often. Most everyone assumes that when someone stares into space they're not paying attention. However, they might just be thinking. They might just be thinking about making their idea a reality. In spite of that, what happens when an idea becomes a reality? Does it just disappear? Vanish from your head completely? Furthermore, what happens when one gets tired of a reality? Does it fly back into your head, transforming back into a simple idea, or does it just fade out to nothingness? What happens when one has no ideas? Are all their ideas realities, or are there no ideas and no realities? What if no one had any ideas? Would our city be here right now? Would the state be here? What about the country? The continent? The planet? The galaxy? The universe? Would

I even be here? I suppose I wouldn't. I probably wouldn't even be here if I, Katie, didn't have any ideas. But what kinds of ideas do I have? Do I have good ones or bad ones? Do I have thoughts or fleeting notions? Do I even have any ideas for this story? No. Wait, what?

Oh, right, the story. The story! I'm running out of time...too much pressure! I can't think under pressure! Well, I couldn't think anyway. Ugh, this is on the brink of preposterous! Think, Katie, think! What should your story be about? Honestly, I have no idea, but I have to have some ideas! I haven't even started writing yet...

Peaceful, But Broken
Jayleen Castro, age 11

Adam Forrester, former photographer and a predator. The reason I know this is because I was a victim. I was only eleven at the time, but unfortunately, I still remember everything. My name is Hunter Grim. I've spent five years of my life tracking him down. Why, you ask? Because he killed my parents right before my eyes. As days turned to weeks that turned to months, I found him.

I realized a flaw in my plan. Who would believe a sixteen-year-old girl found her parents' murderer after five years? They'd think it was a prank. So I have to prove that Adam Forrester is a predator. I found his accounts on dating websites. I created ten different accounts; nine were adults, and one was a teenager. After chatting on all the accounts, Adam Forrester accepted the false teenager. After three weeks of chatting, we decided to hook up. We went for dinner and he invited me to his place. After talking for a while, Adam went to sleep. After twenty minutes had passed, he woke up. By that time, I had him tied up and taped his mouth. How? You may ask? He didn't realize that I had drugged him. He looked confused and tried to yell, but I quickly ran to cover his mouth.

"Hey I'm being nice so stop screaming!" I said, and he stopped struggling.

I rolled him to the master bedroom. He looked as if to say, "Why are you doing this?"

I just smiled and started looking through his things to see if I could find any mementos of his past victims. I found nothing, so I started to circle around him chuckling and said, "They always get caught, Adam."

"Who are you talking about?" he asked.

"You know, Adam, you know."

"I don't," he answered. "Who are you talking about?"

I went to his face and yelled, "The pedophiles, Adam, the pedophiles!"

His facial expression changed. Then I knew he figured out why I was here.

"I don't know what you're talking about," he mumbled.

I chuckled and said, "Yes, you do. Let me tell you a story, Adam. Do you remember a frightened eleven year old seeing her parents killed in front of her? Does that ring a bell?" I asked.

"I don't know," he answered.

I just wanted him to be honest with me and admit what he had done. Suddenly, there was a knock at the door. It was his sister so I quickly pushed him to the restroom. When I returned to the restroom, he was gone and the window was open. I went outside and luckily, he didn't get too far.

He put down the knife he found and said, "I know I have… well a history. I'm sorry, ok?"

"You will never feel what I felt having someone you love taken away right in front of you.

He cried, "Please let me go!"

I told him I would if he confessed to me the events that took place when he killed my parents. He agreed, but he didn't know that he was being recorded. After his confession, I called the police and told them I caught my parents' killer. When they arrived, I gave them Adam and the recording.

I am glad to say now Adam has been given a life sentence.

I have peace of mind followed by a broken heart.

Winds of Winter
Emily Chapin, age 12

The snowflakes flutter to the ground like a teardrop creasing down someone's rosy cheeks. As they land like a fluffy cloud on the ground, they create a wide, never-ending ocean of white. I look out the icy window. All I can see is the slightest bit of tree bark and the streetlights reflecting off the snow, back into my eyes. The chilling winds of winter knock on my door. I can't help but refuse because of the fire's warmth and beauty.

No me Doy Cuenta
Abigail Chevez, age 13

Todos los días, al salir afuera, en verdad no tomo un segundo vistazo al hermoso paisaje frente a mí.

No me doy cuenta de que asombrosas se ven las rosas carmesí.

No me doy cuenta de cómo el sol alumbra a los ríos y lagos, hasta los charcos, haciéndolos ver como si son hechos de diamantes blancos, reluciendo tan bellamente col los rayos del sol.

No me doy cuenta que hermoso el cielo nocturno es. Con su fusión de colores infinitos: azul, rosa, purpura todos mezclados juntos para crear una obra maestra.

No me doy cuenta de que divina se ve la puesta del sol con su mezcla de colores cálidos.

No me doy me cuenta de que encantador se ve el océano azul.

Llevando tesoros desconocidos y ofreciendo la vida a una variedad de criaturas, algunas que la humanidad ha de descubrir.

No me doy cuenta de cómo los arboles están tan altos sobre mí, como gigantes.

Todos los días, al salir afuera, en verdad no noto el paisaje frente a mí.

I Don't Notice (No me Doy Cuenta Translation)

Every day, when I step outside, I don't really take a second look at the remarkable scenery right in front of me.

I don't notice how breathtaking the dark, crimson red roses are.

I don't notice how the sun shines on the rivers and lakes, or even a puddle, making them look like they're made out of white diamonds shining ever so beautifully with the rays of the sun.

I don't notice how beautiful the night sky is.

With its fusion of infinite colors: blue, pink, purple all blended together to create a masterpiece.

I don't notice how divine the sunset looks with its mixture of warm colors.

I don't notice how delightful the blue ocean looks.

Carrying unknown treasures and providing life to a variety of creatures, some humanity has yet to discover.

I don't notice how the trees stand tall, hovering over me like giants.

Every day, when I step outside, I don't really notice the remarkable scenery right in front of me.

Turn it Off in Class
Jaime Clara, age 13

In today's modern world, people own at least one electronic device. Permitting these devices could have many consequences in the academic classroom.

An iPad is one of the many different devices that can distract the learning environment. In reading class, for example, the common excuse could be, "I use it to read." But who knows how many levels they've passed during silent reading time? In math class, the teacher may wonder how the kid got so smart. Well, maybe because there's a calculator on pretty much every electronic device. That's all the "studying" the student claims to have done over the weekend. The student could also come "prepared" for Social Studies by typing in a couple of things in the "Notes" feature.

The most common device used today is the cell phone. It doesn't matter what brand, but almost everybody has one. Back to the example of the calculator, the phone can help cheat in a math test. And phones usually have internet, so the student can Google harder questions. Because of its size compared to the iPad, phones are easier to hide under a desk to play or text during the time to write an essay in English class. While the science teacher plays a video, the student might as well watch a YouTube video of his own. Also, if the phone rings, it can be distracting.

Electronic devices in the classroom can be distracting to the student and the whole class. There can be many excuses for bringing them to class, but what are they really for besides learning? What a student does in class relies on what he or she takes to the classroom. Start by leaving the electronics. That is the first step to a higher success possibility.

Bandana
Louise Cohen, age 12

Blossom
Ellie Consolvo, age 12

Flower Abigale Sethan was a young girl just at the age of six. Flower had the I.Q. of a genius fourteen-year-old. She noticed everything and everyone around her, and knew practically everything important in life, always surpassing her parent's expectations. Well, at least her dad's. Her mother had died when Flower was just at the age of two, due to cancer.

Flower was always a confident girl, but did not understand her name. She was constantly wondering why she was named Flower and not a flower's name. For example: Lily, Rose, or Daisy. The name Flower just did not make sense.

So one day, Flower decided to ask her father why her name was Flower and her dad started off with a heavy sigh. "Well, Flower, when you were born you had these bright, blue eyes that your mother and I knew held so much potential. We knew you would exceed the goals you would be given in life; we knew you would blossom into something beautiful, and that's why your name is Flower." Her dad finished in a whisper.

And that was when she finally understood. She finally knew why her name was Flower, because she would blossom into a successful adult. She would blossom into inspiration that would change the world, and she did.

She grew up to be a successful singer whose songs inspired others. Her lyrics told of memories she loved and hated, both beautiful. Everyone loved her and she was happy with her life and career.

Flower grew older and had two kids with a man named Scott. She and Scott grew old together and also had a girl Mastiff named Bloom. Flower then became old and retired, but still did volunteer work, though no one forgot her name or music. Then the time came and Flower joined her mother. However, the name Flower lived on forever.

Zentangle
Alina Coulter, age 11

Anarchy
Tyla-Simone Crayton, age 11

So imagine a world with no rules, laws, or anything of that sort, but you will still have the laws in science like gravity and other things. When you first think about it, you might think it's awesome. For example, you think you can get everything for FREE, you can be rich, you don't have to have an education to get a job, you don't have to go to school, you don't have to teach if you don't what to, and more. But there are also many bad things that you didn't think about like there would be CHAOS, there would be no jail, you would not have to take a driving test to drive, you wouldn't have to be twenty-one to drink, you don't have to have a license to apply for a credit card, stealing would be allowed, there would be a lot of killing, fires, robbing, no protection from the government, and more. So anarchy can be bad and good if you think about it, but it is mostly bad.

Pagani Huayra
Joseph Dibsi, age 12

Laws: Unfair and Unjust?
Lauren Dotson, age 13

Is there a time when it is better to break law/rule? If so, when?

No, it's never good to break the law, but there are good reasons to break the law. Laws are meant to be followed, but sometimes they are not always fair. In this paper, I will explain some of the few laws that are better to be broken.

Here are some of the traffic laws that are better to be broken and the ones that you absolutely *have* to break (no question). Like when your wife is in labor and you need to speed to the hospital. You'll still have to go to court, but you likely won't get a ticket. This would also include when someone is dying, or something is wrong with them and they need to be rushed to the hospital. That's a good reason to break the law. Or you could think about when slavery was still around, and you were a slave and your lifelong dream was to be free. That's a great reason to break the law and flee to the north (of the U.S.A). Have you noticed these are emergency reasons? None of these reasons are like, I felt like walking on the street just because (jaywalking ticket). Another time you might be forced to break the law is when an ambulance is going by. Even if you are at a red light, it's okay to move because the ambulance has to get by. So you wouldn't get a ticket if you were to move (which you kind of have to if a life is in danger). This is a reason from which you can sometimes benefit, because if you let the ambulance go, you don't have to wait either.

You could also have good reasons to break a law in another country. Like in Afghanistan, they don't let women wear pants or they would be killed on the spot. These are very unfair laws because people should be able to wear anything they want and not be judged. There is another unfair law in Saudi Arabia: it states it's illegal for a woman to drive an automobile. This is really unfair. Going back to what I said, all people have rights and no one can take those away. When reading certain paragraphs, I found some proof. It states in The Great Ideas chapter 46 LAW: laws in which God implants in human nature do not differ in their eternal origin in the divine intellect and will, or in the manifestation of the divine government of the world. This states that all people are equal and that's the way it should be.

These were some of the few laws that are unfair in the past and the present. I know that someday these laws will be fixed, but for now, our world isn't all the way at peace. And as long as there is man on earth we will have more problems even after some are fixed.

The Unknown Man
Lauren Dotson, age 13

I looked around, bewildered as I sat in my cold, hard chair. On my desk it said I was chief police officer, but I didn't remember a thing. I guarded my emotions, as I sat still with my face straight. I felt lethargic as if someone gave me a sleeping pill. Almost restless as my surroundings swirled in and out of focus. I couldn't understand why. I could hear a man outside the door elated about something I didn't know. In front of me were papers I had filled out, but I knew at this moment I had another job. Maybe not a job that I could fulfill on my own this time.

There was a knock at the door. "May I come in?" the rough, deep voice said.

I called back, "Yes," knowing I had to face whatever happened next. I couldn't stay here forever. Maybe it wasn't the smartest choice but it was all I had left. A man dressed in a butler's suit walked in carrying a tray of assorted drinks.

"Sir, the president requests your presence, please follow me."

I got up out of my chair and started to follow him. I noticed blood dripping down my leg, cold and deep red. There were bullet holes all over me, but amazingly, I didn't feel anything. I hadn't noticed it before, so why was it there and how did it get there? I started to tremble and shake with unbearable shock.

I could hear the butler saying, "Sir, please get up. We must go see the president."

I hadn't even felt myself falling towards the ground, what was happening to me? That was the last thing I heard and then I woke up in a dark room, sitting in a chair.

My hands and feet were tied up and I was cold. Where was I? I heard a man whisper in the distance.

"Shh... He's awake." A man walked from the darkness and said, "Phillip Gabe Thompson, you have done some bad things."

He pulled out a gun and started talking once more, "You have something of ours and unless you give it back I am going to shoot you."

My mind was running wild with questions. *What do I have? Why do they need it? My name is Phillip? I can't die now!*

I mumbled back stronger than I felt, "I am sorry but I don't have what you need."

He said, "Excuse me, but I don't think it's smart to talk back to a man with a gun threatening to end your life."

He shot me once in the leg. Sweating, I screamed in agony as I watched more blood drip down my leg. He kept shooting and then everything went blank.

A rosy red color filled my head then a blank white took its place. I awoke startled, but okay next to my wife.

"IT WAS A DREAM!" I yelled with glee as I kissed my wife.

"Shhhh......," my wife said, "You'll wake the children."

I kissed her again and I fell back asleep happy and relieved.

As I fell back into to a deep, dark, fulfilling sleep, I thought I heard, "This isn't over," with a bloodcurdling chuckle.

The Mutated Massacre
Damian Drabek, age 12

This was honestly getting boring, I sighed as I stepped out of the factory. Ten years ago, I started here. I'm getting promoted. Nothing major like manager or anything. Just upgrading to waste management. I went home that day and turned on the TV.

"Today a strange chemical, T-125, spilled through the sewer chambers at The New York Waste Management facility on Varick Avenue in Brooklyn early this morning...," said the news anchor.

"Hey, that's where I work," I whispered under my breath. "Oh no! "I mumbled. "I should go check it out."

As I walked through the intersections, I noticed the C.D.C.—the Contagious Disease Control—and they had suits with vacuum looking things. I quickly scurried to the waste room. It was empty and there was nothing in sight like my mom and her O.C.D.—something you don't expect at *waste* management is a clean room. I jumped from the catwalk into the Pit. There was a big hole that went into the sewer chambers.

Should I go in there or not? I pondered.

I thought if I went in, I would have gotten lost. I tried to stay out of the way, keep my head down, and just do my job and clock out. Later, I went back to my apartment.

"We have reports of people getting sick from some type of smoke from the sewers. We advise people to stay inside"

"Could it be?" I whispered to myself.

I quickly looked out my window and saw a red fog and a man on the ground gasping for air. Then he started to change into something inhuman with his skin falling off his bones, and trying to rip his own face off. I tried not to look, but it was as if I was a deer in headlights.

"Close the window," my subconscious said.

Then he started to run around like a headless chicken throwing and destroying anything in its path. That's when I heard screaming from outside my door in the hallway. I wondered if I should go check it out, but I was too scared. Finally, I manned up and checked. As I opened my door slowly and peered out, I saw what looked like my neighbor, Josh, only it wasn't really him. His face was contorted, his skin sagging off his bones, and dripping in blood and what looked like slime.

"Oh God, Josh," I whispered to myself.

He was running after Mrs. Margeri and her baby from 3C. As soon as I heard the scream and the baby crying, I ran to my closet and reloaded my double barrel shotgun in the blink of an eye. I then ran outside and shot him in the chest and the head. That was when it teleported! At least that's what I think it did. It just hit the ground, then a blue flash came and it was gone. That is when I hauled Mrs. Margeri up and put her in her apartment while she was shaking and crying, I asked if the baby was all right and she didn't answer. I told her to stay inside and bolt her door shut. I had to find out what was going on, so I went and got all my extra ammo, got into my car and took off. I got to the factory, and there were infected scientists everywhere. Then, they attacked me from behind! I managed to kill one, but I ran from the others. As I walked through the side doors, I noticed light corning from the crack in the chamber. I jumped in the crack to see a tunnel full of light! I walked to the end and found a lab, but it was torn up. As I walked through the lab, I heard a bunch of "Zaps." I kept walking, and that's when I heard people. They were busy doing something on the other side, so I walked quietly to the door. I accidentally hit it with my shotgun, and then the scientist hit a red button, the door closed behind me, and then a red fog immersed the room. A voice said the T-125 was being released. I couldn't breathe. It was like fire in my lungs and in my eyes. I fell to the ground choking. I tried crawling, but blacked out within minutes. I managed to wake up, and to my surprise I was alive. That's when the scientist opened the door. He dragged me into the office, but I was fine, no saggy bones, no green slime. So then I stood up, and there were blue flashes everywhere. Then I remembered the teleporting from the apartment. I ran to the door and the scientist saw me. He looked very stunned.

He took me in and said, "You got infected. How did you not

change?"

That's when I said, "I think I am immune. I guess working at the factory for ten years with hazardous waste will do that."

That's when the scientist took my blood sample and made the cure for the infection. They fogged the whole city a purple hew and said it was for the mosquitoes. They stopped the infection, and the Varick facility was mysteriously burned to the ground. Everyone was cured and New York was saved.

Le Cupcake
Shelby Edison, age 12

1 My name is Olivia LeCeen (le-seen) and I love cupcakes. I know that a lot of people say that they love cupcakes, but I am the cupcake queen. I live in New York, but I am originally from France. Paris to be exact. My family owns a cupcake bakery here called *Le Cupcake*. I work there on the weekends with my sister, Jacqueline or Jackie for short, who is 3 years younger than me. Here in New York, I go to Green High School. I'm in the 10th grade. I have a teacher named Miss Candy. Don't let the name confuse you. She is like baking a cupcake and adding salt instead of sugar. I am not her biggest fan. Neither are my three BFFs: Camille, Elouise, and Virginia. I moved here in the 6th grade and they right away became my best friends. We always stick together. We all have a certain characteristic that identifies us in the group. I'm the baker, Camille is the crafter, Virginia is the sporty one, and Elouise is the tech nerd (and genius). We always say that our skills are what will allow us to survive the zombie apocalypse. It's around Christmas time, my favorite time of the year. The special holiday flavors at *Le Cupcake* are fabulous and creating them is even better. My favorite part is decorating the shop with tinsel and lights in the shape of cupcakes, of course! My weekend will go something like this: wake up, go to *Le Cupcake*, invent and bake cupcakes, manage the store, go home and walk my dog, Mac (a French bulldog), eat lunch, bake more cupcakes, eat dinner, sleep. It is exhausting. Sometimes my friends will come over and we can chat. They'll even help serve. So far, this system works really well. And if homework allows, I might even have time to curl up by the fire in *Le Cupcake* and read a good book. And, of course, it is a French pastry book called *Le Luxe Francais Patisserie Cookbook*. Yes, it is in French. I have thought about expanding *Le Cupcake* to make it all pastries, but my mother says that it is too risky. Many people may not like the other treats. My father says that we would have to rename the shop *Le*

Pastries. Jackie says that macaroons are too hard to make. But I am determined to make my dream come true one day.

 I rolled out of bed Saturday morning. I heard a sound. Elevator music. I glanced at the clock. 8:49 a.m.

I grabbed my phone and texted Jackie: "I will get back at you."

Apparently, Jackie had stayed up late and switched the buzzer on my alarm to elevator music. The shop opened at 10 a.m. I was late. I needed to get to the bakery as fast as possible. I slipped on jeans, a blue longed sleeve shirt, boots, and a hot pink beret. The beret is my signature fashion piece. Then I crawled into a *Le Cupcake* hoodie that said *Le Cupcake* on the front and "Don't mess with me, I bake cupcakes," on the back. I grabbed my apron and ran out the door to hop on my bike and get myself to *Le Cupcake.* I burst through the door of *Le Cupcake* and gave Jackie an evil glance. My mom looked at me.

"Cette chose mal mis mon alerte," I explained while looking in Jackie's direction. This meant, "That evil thing switched my alarm." Jackie had forgotten some French with the transition to America. I wasn't sure how, but I used it to my advantage.

My mom responded, "Je vais prendre soin d'elle plus tard. Aller cisson." This meant, "I'll take care of her later. Go bake."

I did as I was told and went into the kitchen. If you had never been into the *Le Cupcake* kitchen, it would be like entering a whole other world. Pots, pans, wrappers, muffin tins, pastry bags, and all sorts of ingredients covered the countertops like blankets of fresh snow. Piles of flour and sugar would form on your hands if you slid them across the table. Photocopies of recipes lined the walls and chances were, that if you were there on a daily basis, you would step on a fair share of them. To sum it up, the *Le Cupcake* kitchen is a wonderland. And in the winter, it was even better. We blasted Christmas carols in the kitchen and holiday smells like peppermint and nutmeg would find their way into your nose. My dad was already working on the gingerbread cupcake batter and the lemon- blueberry ones were in the oven. I got to work on the peppermint twist cupcake. I pulled out the peppermint extract that was set high on the extract shelf and was only pulled out once a year. My father and I used to joke that we would need nose plugs for it because if the scent went into our nostrils we would lose our sense of smell. That was how strong it was. And also the reason it was only used once a year. I braced myself as I twisted open the lid. The smell of peppermint filled the room. My dad coughed. Jackie started to walk into the kitchen, then recoiled as she smelled the extract.

"Are you almost done with that stuff?" she asked. But, her nose was plugged, so it sounded more like, "Whare you whalmost done whith that stwuff?"

I shook my head and she ran out of the room, her turtle neck covering her nose and mouth. I took out the 1/8 of a teaspoon measuring cup and dripped a few drops of the peppermint into it. I poured it into the bowl and quickly twisted the lid back on.

"Jackie, you can come back in," I said. The peppermint is sealed and put away." Under my breath I added, "Until tomorrow."

She came back into the kitchen and started to whip up some frosting and make super cute gingerbread men out of fondant for the tops of the gingerbread cupcake. I continued stirring and added ingredients to the peppermint twist batter. I occasionally glanced over at Jackie's decorations. After completing my batter, I pulled a piece of paper out of my apron pocket. I slid it over near my sister's work space.

"What's this?" she asked.

"This is a picture of holly leaves. I thought that it could top the eggnog cupcake nicely," I responded.

"You want paper on top of cupcakes?" she asked, being an annoying sister.

"Made of fondant," I said while hardly moving my lips. *Comment vais-je meme raconte a ma soeur? (How am I even related to my sister?)* I said to myself.

Yes, I love Jackie, but, like any little sister, she has a talent to get on my nerves 24/7. I finished spooning cupcake batter into the tins and set them in the oven. After another hour of intense cupcake baking, I started to set them up in the display case and prepare the shop for today's visitors. I walked into the restroom and washed the flour out of my hair. I washed my hands trying to remove traces of red food coloring I used for the peppermint twist cupcakes. I cleaned off my apron and went to the front desk, ready to serve customers. The first customer walked in.

"Hello. Welcome to *Le Cupcake*. What can I get for you today?" I said to the customer.

The girl who had walked in studied the menu. She peered into the display case. Her eyes dashed back and forth between options. Finally, she opened her mouth to order.

"I'll take a double chocolate delight cupcake and a caramel latte," she said.

"Certainly, that'll be $6.72," I said with a smile.

The lady smiled back and handed me some cash. I fingered it and smiled again. I had just gotten one dollar and 28 cents as a tip. Smiling is a trick I learned from my mom. In 6th grade, when I wasn't allowed to work at the counter yet, I would watch my mother. She would greet the customer, suggest options, take the money, and give the customer their order, all while smiling. She would put some money in the cash register and she would finger some money and slide it into her apron. One day I asked her, "Are those tips people are giving you?"

"Yes, they are," my mother said.

That same year, my father hired my cousin who lived in Italy to help out. I would watch her too. She would put far less money into her apron. Later, I asked my mom, "Why does Kate get less tips than you when you do the same thing?"

My mom bent down and whispered in my ear, "I smile. It's the key to tips. People tip people who smile."

These are some words of wisdom that I hear in my head every single time someone walks into the store. I gave the lady her cupcake and told her that I would bring her latte to her. I didn't like the latte machine. It was complicated. It was also an Italian machine, so the instructions were in Italian and the pictures were impossible to read. To me, it looked like pigs coming out of a flying saucer holding coffee mugs. I fiddled with a few buttons, pulled some leavers, added the coffee beans, and hoped that the thing worked. It rumbled and brown liquid flowed into the mug. I breathed a breath of relief. I handed the lady her latte and started to serve other customers that walked through the door, I called to my father to help me with the counter. He walked in and helped me with orders. I still hadn't seen any of my friends, but I knew that they would come soon. They better. I stood there serving cupcakes and coffee for about an hour or two. Finally, I saw a familiar face. I could see the blond top of Elouise's head, her hair flung carelessly around her shoulder. She had so many tall people in front of her, I wasn't sure it was even her. But then she came closer and I saw that it was 100% Elouise.

"What can I get for you?" I asked.

She smiled, looked down at a list in her hand, and started to speak, "I'll take one eggnog cupcake, two viper vanilla cupcakes, and one gingerbread cupcake in a box. And one peppermint twist cupcake with a peppermint hot cocoa on the side for me." She took a huge breath.

"That'll be $17.64. What do you need all those cupcakes for anyways?" I asked Elouise.

"My mom's having company over tonight. She wanted to bake dessert, but I said I was coming over here anyways and I would just buy some cupcakes. Besides, my mother plus baking equals disaster," she told me.

I handed Elouise her cupcakes and she went to sit down. After pushing five million buttons on the latte machine, I finally was able to give Elouise her hot cocoa. I handed her the mug with the creamy, sweet hot cocoa in it and returned behind the desk.

"Va se amuser avec Elouise. Je peax gerer le compteur," my dad said to me. I smiled a very wide grin. He had just told me that I could have fun with Elouise and he could manage the counter.

I ran over to Elouise's table. "What are you doing today, Ellie?" I asked her.

"Nothing, why?" she asked. I started to squeal like a little girl. I explained how I could spend the day with her and I didn't have to work at *Le Cupcake*. I love working at the cupcake shop, but I would rather be doing other things this weekend. For example, hanging out with Elouise. I was in the middle of chatting with Elouise when... a costumer walked through the doors. Her brown hair was put in a bun on top of her head and she wore a red t-shirt, black skinny jeans, and black high-heeled mini-boots. She was none other than Miss Candy, my dreaded history teacher. Now, by just describing her, I am not giving you justice to the evilness of her. Miss Candy is horrific. She doesn't let you sit next to your friends. If you merely cough during her lesson, she will scream at you for talking during class. Just smiling at a friend will get you blamed for passing notes. And putting your hair back during class, now that is unacceptable. She will say to you, and I quote, "This is school, not a beauty salon." So when Miss Candy walks into *Le Cupcake*, I run away. Usually, I am working at the counter and I can easily sneak into the kitchen. This time, I am at a table. If I try to sneak into the kitchen, she will see me. To make matters worse, I can't even try. My parents put a strict "No guests in the kitchen during business hours" or "Aucun client de la kitachen pendant les heures d'affaires" rule. My parents would not make an exception to that rule for me to escape being seen by my teacher. I had one choice left.

"Follow me. Quickly," I told Elouise.

Keeping the back of my head towards Miss Candy, I quickly made my way into the ladies room. Elouise was right behind me. We were relieved. Until we heard high heel clops coming to the bathroom. I dragged Elouise into a stall and shut the purple door behind us. I switched the latch so that the stall was locked. I breathed heavily. *Bang, clang!* It was the sound of a stall door closing and locking. I unlocked the stall door and ran with Elouise out of the restroom back to our table. We giggled to ourselves. Everything was going our way for about five minutes until my evil teacher walked out of the restroom. I signaled for Elouise to run with me to the counter and to my advantage, Jackie was there.

"Hi, Elouise. Why are you back here? It's is staff only..." Jackie started to say.

"Keep her here for a minute, Jackie," I commanded, cutting her off.

Elouise smiled at me. She turned her head towards the coffee machine and pretended like she worked there and was making coffee. I passed her my apron and she swiftly put it on. Elouise was a genius. She looked exactly like *Le Cupcake* staff. I ran into the kitchen and grabbed some sunglasses and a hat for Elouise from the locker bench. The "locker bench" is our locker room where we leave belongings while we work. I was wearing my beret, so I didn't need a hat. I ran out of the kitchen and we both put on the sunglasses. She wore the hat. We were disguised. I have never wanted to get out of *Le Cupcake* as much as right then. After successfully getting myself and Elouise to the sidewalk, I saw something flying in the sky. This particular thing happened to be falling out of the sky in the direction of my head, which it hit. I looked down. It was a ball that hit me, a soccer ball with the words "Virginia Mill" written on it in black Sharpie.

"Sorry," a voice called out.

Virginia stood in front of me. She was wearing sweatpants and a sweatshirt that said Green High School Soccer on it. Her brown hair was tied back behind her head. I handed her back her ball.

"Thanks," she said.

We started to walk down the sidewalk and we chatted as we walked.

"Did you hear what the all school musical is this year?" I asked.

Elouise and Virginia shook their heads.

"The Wizard of Oz!" I spilled.

"What part do you want? Probably not Dorothy, right?" Virginia said to me.

"Why not Dorothy?" I asked. "I am Dorothy Gale from Kansas," she said in a terrible French accent.

"You can't be French and from Kansas at the same time."

She was right. Virginia is a great friend, but she always tells the truth, whether you like it or not. Last year had been perfect. The musical had been *Beauty and the Beast*. I was the ideal image for Belle. I had the French accent and the brown hair that shouted Belle. I sighed. I'd hopefully find some tech job to do. We found Camille sitting on a park bench reading. She was a bookworm.

"Hi," I said.

"Oh hey, didn't see you," Camille said.

Virginia gave a look that said, "Obviously you didn't see us, your eyes were stuck in the pages of a book."

The day went by fast. It wasn't until 2 p.m. that Camille got the craving to go into a bookstore, so we headed to the nearest one called *Bookworm*. Camille walked through the aisles then found a book and sat right there on the floor with her face completely covered by the mask of the book. I walked over to the cooking section. I pulled a French pastry cookbook off the shelf. My eyes looked longingly at the pictures of macaroons, éclairs, croissants, and so much more. I could smell the sweet aromas. I could picture myself whipping up batters. Then I got an idea. And unlike the Grinch, it was a wonderful, fantastic, splendid idea.

3   I hurried home and ran up to my room. I sat at my desk, pulled out some paper and a pen, and started to write. I was writing to Aunt Marie. She lived in Paris and owned a cheese shop, *Fromage*. She was very well known for her selection of artisan cheeses. Many famous chefs came to her shop to buy the finest cheese for their fancy dishes. She went to culinary school and knew about all sorts of cooking. If I could convince her to convince my parents that selling more than cupcakes at *Le Cupcake* is a good idea, then I am pretty sure that my parents would listen and be convinced that we could sell all sorts of pastries at *Le Cupcake*. It would take a lot of convincing, but I was going to try. What's the harm in that? I quickly sealed the letter up and tossed in the mailbox. "Safe travels," I whispered to the letter.

On Monday, I hurried to theatre. I wasn't excited. We were planning the musical and I obviously wasn't cut out to be Dorothy. I planned to be stage manager, which wasn't a bad job. I just preferred to be on stage. Ms. Conte, our theatre teacher walked into the classroom.

"Okay class, what parts are we interested in for the musical?" she said cheerfully.

Kelsey Healy raised her hand and said, "I was thinking that maybe I could do costumes."

Ms. Conte thought about it for a minute. "Sounds good," she said.

I raised my hand meekly. "I guess I'll do stage hand," I said.

"Are you sure? You always love to act. I was thinking that you could star as the villain. After all, you love to sing," Ms. Conte said.

I was puzzled. "The Wicked Witch of the West doesn't sing," I said.

Now it was Ms. Conte's turn to be puzzled. "Wicked Witch of the West? We are doing the Little Mermaid and last time I checked, Ursula is the villain. She sings," she explained.

"Oh, I thought that we were doing the Wizard of Oz, well oops," I said.

Before class was over, we had gotten our scripts and I was already pulling out my hot pink highlighter and highlighting Ursula's lines.

4 Okay, flash forward a week, and let's take a look at my life. I am practicing very, very hard to perfect Poor Unfortunate Souls. The play is right after break and I want everyone to remember the villain. I'm not going to lie, this part is hard. I've never been an evil squid/octopus who lives in an undersea lair, so the part is hard to relate to. I've messed up my scene in rehearsal so many times because my tentacles are so hard to control. One second they're next to me and the next they're hitting Flotsam and Jetsam. I've been so caught up with rehearsal, school, and *Le Cupcake*, that I've almost forgotten about the letter I sent to Aunt Marie. That is, until I got home from school. I walked through the door and my French bulldog, Mac came to greet me. Mac's real name is Macaroon after the French pastry, but everyone calls him Mac. I scratched him behind the ears and gave him a gourmet doggy treat (a.k.a. Milk Bone coated in bacon). Then I walked to the kitchen island and noticed an opened envelope sitting smack dab in the middle of it. I read who it was addressed to, me. I had definitely not opened it. I looked at the return address, Marie LeCeen. I pulled out the stationary from the envelope and read:

Dear Olivia,

I was delighted to get your letter. I find that you are an excellent baker/pasty chef and I encourage you to follow your dreams. In response to what your letter said, I believe that selling other pastries at *Le Cupcake* is a great idea. I know that many people will pay an excess amount of money to eat a French pastry. I know that this idea has been discussed with your parents and sister and the response has been no. If I ran the shop, it would have been an automatic yes, but to my dismay, I do not. I do believe one thing; if you are to sell other pastries at *Le Cupcake*, you must have the proper training. I can see no other place better than Paris to obtain such training. I will pay for an entire month of tuition for you to one of the finest culinary schools in Paris and, of course, you may stay with me. Please discuss this idea with your parents, for they will not appreciate me telling them what to do with their daughter. If the answer is no, the battle is not over. Tell your parents to call me and I will discuss the matters with them. I will do as much as I can to get you to Paris this summer. Until we talk again, au revoir!

-Aunt Marie

I stared at the letter. I hadn't meant for it to go this far. I wanted to go to Paris and attend culinary school. That would mean leaving *Le Cupcake* for a while. Although, it would improve *Le Cupcake*. My mind was racing. Then my mom and dad entered the room.

"Vous avez ouvert lat lettre, ne avez-vous?" I said. (You opened the letter didn't you?)

My mom and dad looked at each other and then my mother sighed "Oui." (Yes) I wanted to know more. "Et..." I said. (And...) My father finished, "Nous approuvons. We approve." He said it in French and English to make sure I understood.

I smiled. Some parts of the battle had been won, but I had a long path in front of me before I reached the finish line.

Pastry Face-Off
Shelby Edison, age 12

Every Thursday night at 8:00 pm, I watch *Pastry Face-Off* on the *Food Channel*. The show starts with its theme song: "Make it, bake it, decorate it, on *Pastry Face-Off!*" Then it shows the contestants. I never dreamed that one day I would be on that screen after the theme song played.

My name is Ginger Juniper. With a name like that, it seems I am destined to bake. I have been trying to convince my parents for the last year and a half that baking is what I want to do for the rest of my life. But, they want me to become an engineer even though my math average is a C+. My parents own a bookstore, *Juniper Books*. So, I don't see why it is so far-fetched for me to bake, since they chose to own a bookstore instead of becoming engineers. Maybe it is the career my parents never had so they want it for me. All that this expectation has been doing is torturing me. Should I pursue happiness for my parents or myself? I knew that my parents wouldn't give in easily, but I also knew that I wasn't going to become an engineer, so how could the news be broken to them? That's when I got the idea to complete the *Pastry Face-Off* application. Before I submitted it, I used a pseudonym, Katrina York, just in case any mail came back from the studio. To my surprise, a letter came back inviting me to be on the show.

The studio was only 20 minutes away from my school so I could easily hop on a bus to get there. I knew that my parents wouldn't be happy, but it came down to how I wanted to live *my* life, not the life my parents wanted me to live. Before I knew it, the day of the competition arrived. The bell rang and I anxiously ran out of school and caught the bus to the studio. During the ride, I looked over the cupcake recipes I had brought with me. I planned on making Strawberry Supreme Cupcakes, a recipe I created myself. Although I was a little nervous about baking against professional pastry chefs, I would try my best. While waiting in the backstage area, before show time, I called my mom and left this message, "Hi, it's me Ginger. I have a tutorial after school and I'll be late for dinner. Can you please record *Pastry Face-Off* for me? Thanks." It was a little white lie, but if she checked the channel, she would see me. Before the show started, I slid my phone into my pocket and walked onto the set.

It was a dream come true. The amount of sweets was unbelievable and excitement ran through my veins. As I waited for the host to finish explaining the rules, my phone vibrated. I checked it and found a text from my mom. It read: "Good luck! I know that you'll do great. We believe in you!" Now, it didn't matter if I won. My bakery is out there somewhere, waiting for the day I post the open sign to *Ginger's Sweet Treat Shoppe*.

The Wakeup Call
Robert Ellis III, age 12

Hi, my name is Daniel Richardson and this is a story about the time I lost my brother, John, and it changed my life. I was a bad kid back then. I failed classes, talked back to my parents and teachers, and I even slapped my mom once. Back then, I didn't really care about anything except my little brother and basketball. Those seemed to be my only interests in life.

Basketball was my interest because I was the best player in the neighborhood. Of course, I couldn't play at school because of my grades, but that didn't stop me. My brother on the other hand, was the opposite of me. He did well in school and took life how he *wanted* it, not how it was. That was what made my day a little better. But he soon died because of my stupid actions. This is how it happened.

It was a sunny day and I just got back from school with a bunch of homework I decided not to do. Instead, I went to play basketball outside in the driveway. John was out there too with his chalk, sitting on the patio drawing stick figures of the dad he never saw, the mother that was on crack, and his brother, me. It was sad seeing that he had no idea of any of this stuff, but I guess it was for the best. I went to play basketball, practicing my shots and handles when I missed an easy shot. I was astonished to see that I missed it and that it rolled out in the street, but even more astonished to see my brother run after it. As he was running, I tried to tell him to watch out for the car that was coming, but it was too late. A car had ran him over. As I saw his body along with the pool of blood, I didn't know what to do. He was the only one I'd cared about and now he's gone and it's all my fault for not doing what I was supposed to be doing. And then I stood there, waiting for him to get up, even though I knew in the back of my mind that he was dead.

Words couldn't really describe how I felt that day. I was too young to start a new life, so I ran. Not knowing where I was going, I was stopped by an old lady who took me in despite what I had told her about my life. Her nice, smooth, gentle voice reminded me of my brother's. I had no idea that other people were special like him. So I thought to myself, "If there are people like my brother then maybe, just maybe, I can change myself to have a better life instead of acting like a fool." And on that day forward, I decided to change my life and act like the older brother I was supposed to be.

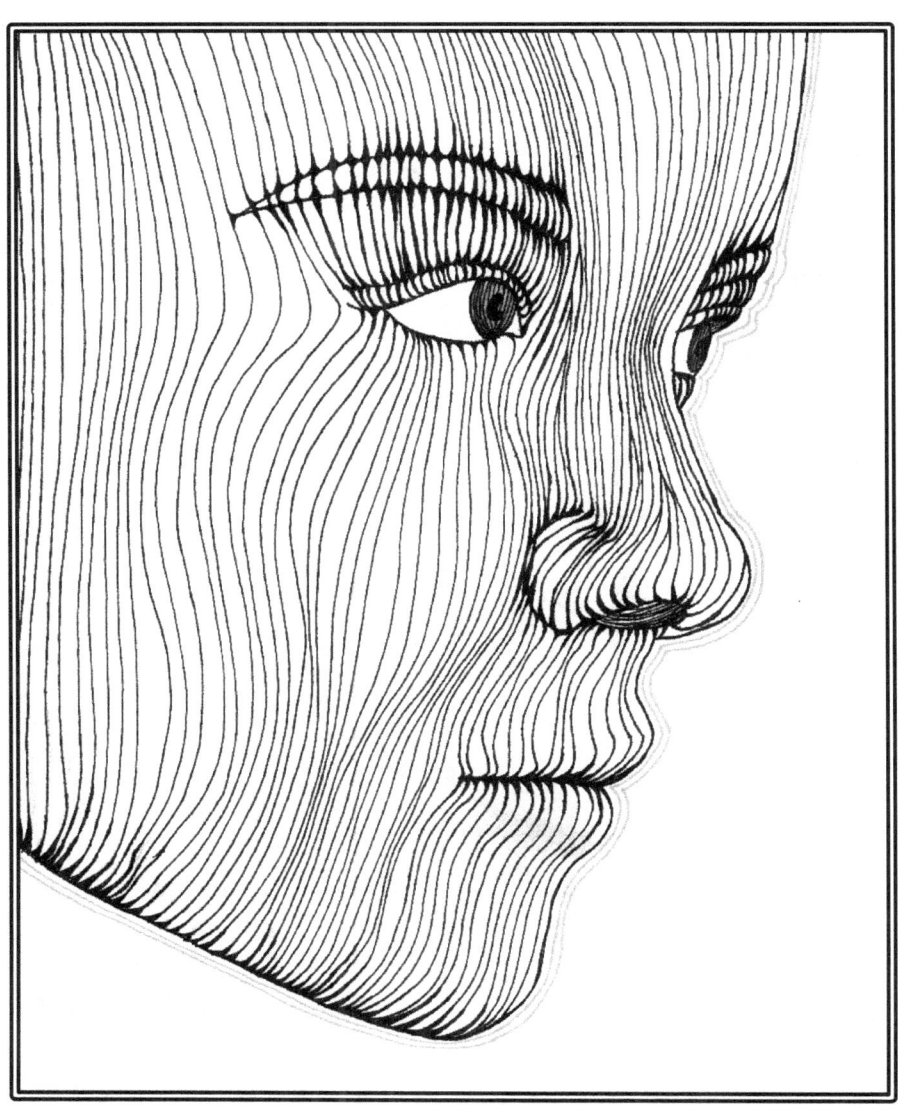

Untitled
Elyse Evans, age 14

Untitled
Elyse Evans, age 14

Untitled
Elyse Evans, age 14

The Ramblings of an Undecided Individual
Emma Fiesinger, age 13

Since it is currently March 12, 2015 (this will probably be a different date when you read this), and I'm supposed to turn it whatever magnificent masterpiece that will revolutionize everyone's way of thinking tomorrow, I can't think of anything to write. Sure, I may have ideas, but they all sound not too good as I think about it more. Because just like skydiving, it's best not to think about what is currently at hand.

I'm surprised the early stages of assignment panic haven't set in. Do I want it to set in? No. Would it be nice if I could stop all of this indecisiveness that I seem to have? Yeah, it really would be. Undecidedness seems to go hand in hand with another form of sporadic word that does not, contrary to popular belief, appear in the dictionary. Quite a disappointment, actually. Also, procrastination. No eighth-grade student can say that they have never had a passport to Procrastination Nation. Well, at least in my case that's true.

Now I bet you expect me to write that I am happy with the way I am, and that I need more self-confidence, but that simply isn't the case. Would it be a cool, yet slightly overdone topic to write about? Yeah. However, people have written enough poems and sung enough songs for me to really delve into the fascinating world of self-confidence.

Figuring out what I'm going to say here is a real pain in the "I-cant-type-it-because-this-writing-piece-is-supposed-to-be-school-appropriate," so I'm just going to type whatever I feel is necessary because it is my story, and you know I'm going to tell it.

It all started on a (supposedly) warm summer Friday. The birds chirped, the sun shone, and the nonexistent ducks quacked. I would love to talk more ABOUT the exciting world of childbirth, but that would include an R-rated warning label for strong language, blood, and violence, and it's a boring topic. Well, my birth (AKA the Birth of Emma the Great and Powerful) wasn't boring, but the general idea of it is.

I'm getting off track, like a train that doesn't run right. Neither do I. Both the train and I make loud noises to alert people of our arrival. I'm beginning to think that I am part train. Time to examine the birth certificate again.

Anyway, I'm going to wrap this up into a neat little package with a neat little bow. Even though you are probably thinking that this was way too short, I hope to expand on this sort of thing in the days of the future. I'd like to thank the Academy.

In all seriousness, I'd like to thank the people who I think really made school worthwhile (I received an education, but that isn't fun). I'm just kidding. Anyways, my friends helped me get through school. Chances are, if I've talked to you more than once with a seemingly positive tone of voice over half the time, I appreciate and value you as a beautiful individual—from coming up with theories of the universe, to arguing over stuff that won't matter when the sun implodes on itself billions (I hope) of years into the future, to beating you in games I should have lost, to accidentally scaring you, to even jostling you to far-off corners of the small slab while you are willingly blinded—you guys have been there for me. I really appreciate it. I hope you look at this when you're old and wrinkly, and you smile to yourself. I hope you whisper, "That crazy Emma, that weird Emma, that one girl that I worried about, that great and awesome Emma, my friend, that Undecided Individual."

Forte and Piano
Prince Frazier, age 12

Forte! Forte! Trumpets blowing, Tuba's booming!

Piano

Piano

Piccolos' lowing

Violins strumming

Fortissimo!

Fortissimo!

Band Blasting

Booming Songs

Pianissimo

Pianissimo

Flutes fluting a sweet song

Misunderstood
Alizey Garcia, age 12

As we sit anxiously awaiting the results of Mikey's test, I frantically wonder what his diagnoses will be. Will he have to take medication? Will we be able to control it? He's been having trouble since the beginning of the year with his first grade teacher, and now that he's been brought to a diagnostician, it's all too real. Sometimes, I wonder what it's like to be in his shoes. I know most of you reading this are probably thinking that I must be such a worry wart and what not, but just imagine having to see a six-year-old boy having to go through all of this. It's not very fun. My mom tells me I need to be more understanding because he is going through tough times which, yes, I know, but what she doesn't understand is that she is not always going be there for him. Finally, the diagnostician comes out and invites us to her surprisingly messy office where she confirms that Mikey has dyslexia! This was very unexpected. We all thought it was an attention problem! As we all look toward the ground, I wonder what everyone is thinking. Busting the silence, my mom asks her what can we do to help him and she says a whole bunch of bundled up words only my parents understand.

It all makes sense now, all of his struggles are explainable. The struggle with spelling, reading, and attention is caused by the dyslexia. Day in and day out, we have taken turns helping Mikey with his homework with no success. He comes back home with thirties and fifties. Fail, fail, and more failing. His conduct isn't any better, P's and U's. Apparently, he doesn't look at the teacher when she is talking, he can't stay still during carpet time, he plays in the bathroom, can't stand in line, and so on and so forth. All of this has caused him to become very anxious and have low self-esteem. Everything has become a struggle from putting on his shoes in the morning to brushing his teeth at night. But now I realize he has just been misunderstood all along. So, I bet you're thinking *what if he fails?* Well, I can answer that. We live on the rough side of town and let's just say were not exactly zoned to the best schools. I don't know one person who has even tried to attend those schools. Children get picked on, kids get pushed. Gangs and drug activity happen daily and he wouldn't have good role models. Right now he currently attends a good, diverse school with high standards, but I wonder if there's room for dyslexic children there, because dyslexics struggle with academics and this school *only* wants the best. If he continues to fail, he's out! ROUGH SCHOOL, HERE WE COME!

As the diagnostician explains all of his accommodations, it sounds to me like we are on a road to recovery. All he needs are reading interventions! We're on our way to a solution to this problem, or so I thought. He gets all the accommodations he needs, but he's failing horribly. He desperately needs help, but everything that we try is not getting anywhere. We've tried a counselor and it has helped a little with his confidence. He also has an outside tutor that cost an arm and a leg. What if nothing ends up working?! I begin to panic and wonder what his future looks like. But then I begin to think, so what if he goes to that run down school? It doesn't mean his life will be a total failure. There is more to him than just "academics!" When it comes to playing and being a normal six year old, he is awesome; he rides his bike, jumps on the trampoline, and he is perfect. Except his self-esteem has dramatically dropped due to his low grades. Everything has been affected by his diagnosis and I feel really bad because school is supposed to be a fun, positive place.

Right now, our dog Daisy is his best friend; he loves her very much. I think Daisy helps him deal with his emotions while he goes through all this. I couldn't imagine life without her. He also knows or is learning how to play basketball and I have to say he is pretty good. Bikes are fun too, and when we race, sometimes he beats me! Unfortunately, being a fun, normal six year old with dyslexia is not what he is tested on at school. Just as we were giving up, his third nine weeks report card came home and to our surprise his grades looked so much better! His grades were not "awesome" but he was passing with seventies. We could not be happier, he worked so hard! We all worked so hard and to think it is finally paying off; the feeling of success is just so awesome! To celebrate his first success we are going to Marble Slab! Slowly but surely, his grades and conduct are improving greatly. On his next report card he is passing with even better grades! My parents have a meeting with his teacher and she informs them that he is getting better every day; his math is improving and he has gone up two reading levels in five months. Honestly, I never thought we would get this far, but we did! I can't wait to see what awaits us in the future.

Here we are again waiting for his test results, but this time Stanford test results. School is out and scores are getting mailed out this week. We check the mail, desperately waiting every day. The mail man just passed and we got his scores! He barely passed, but he passed! Our house is filled with tears of joy, laughter, and smiles. Dyslexia isn't going anywhere but we are learning how to deal with it. This school year has been tough, but it doesn't matter because we have overcome the obstacles! Next school year will be another challenge, but for now, he has saved his spot at the school he deserves to be at!

Bee Careful With the Bee Sting Treatment
Andy Garcia, age 11

Safety first!!! Did you know that bees release a scent when they are in danger in order to attract other bees? Yes, that is how they communicate.

It is painful when you get stung by a bee, so if you are near a bee hive you may want to get out of there as soon as you can. If not, they will communicate with more bees and they will come and sting you as well!

When you get stung by a honey bee, the honey bee will leave a stinger behind, buried deep in your skin! After the bee leaves the stinger behind, your skin will get red and it will hurt a lot! Then your skin swells and you will start to feel your hand getting warmer.

But let me tell you something you probably didn't know: A bee sting can be helpful too! You may say, but how? Well, for example, my dad suffers from a disease called arthritis that hurts your bones. When he has an arthritis attack, he does not go to the doctor. No!! He goes outside to find a bee, yes a bee, to capture it and sting him.

Once he finds it, he grabs it and it stings him on the part that hurts. A few seconds later, the effect of the bee venom starts to react and helps my dad with the pain.

Many people do not know about this, but bee venom is an amazing medicine that can help many people.

So remember, a bee sting can be beneficial, and at the same time painful.

Best·Friends

We're Best Friends, the silliest of friends,
the ones who always laugh,
the ones who say it loud and proud,
"We are the best of the bests!"
Although we are very different,
We are alike down deep inside,
We laugh and play everyday,
And we always know the right things to say,
We will always have our leaps and bounds.
But that is what friendship is all about,
We are not only best friends,
but we are sisters from different Misters
And we never allow the idea of lying.
And we both agree...Dancing is the closest
thing to flying!

ADORA Goodluck ♥ Serianna Hixson

Best Friends
Adora Goodluck, age 12
Serianna Hixson, age 12

Born to Be Wild
Jackson Guite, age 12

"Ring, ring!"

I groaned, as I got up from my bed and looked at my clock. "What? Six-thirty!" Argh, I forgot to turn my alarm off. "Oh well," I said, "at least I can get an early start on the weekend." I walked downstairs, but something was wrong. My dad wasn't at home, and Mom and my little sister were already awake. I sat down to find out what was wrong.

"Hey, Tim," my mom said, "I have to go to a P.T.O. meeting today and your dad has to work, so you have to watch your sister at the zoo."

"What? Why the zoo?" I said.

"Because she has a friend meeting her there," my mom said. "All you have to do is watch her until they come, and then you're done."

"Fine!" I said, whining more than before.

When my mom dropped my sister and me off, I realized that I left my phone at the house. "Oh, well," I said, "probably won't need it." We walked into the zoo and my sister said, "I want to see the monkeys."

"Alright," I said, "but just for a little while"

So we bought popcorn and headed to the monkey cage. My sister was happy when we located the monkey cage, but when I was watching her, one of the monkeys stole my popcorn! "What in the world?" I said looking at my hand, but when I looked back, I didn't see my sister anywhere. I was looking everywhere, but when I heard her voice, I knew where she was. I looked at the cage where the monkeys were. She was walking through the cage! I panicked, so I ran through the bars and into the cage. I almost caught up to her when I slipped on a banana peel. When I got up, I saw she was on the move, so I ran after her. She was headed for the giraffes! When I finally caught up to her, I could not believe my eyes. My crazy sister was climbing up, and sliding down the giraffe necks! Suddenly, one of the giraffes tilted his head up and she landed in the next cage. I had no idea what was in

70

there, until I heard the roar. I bolted over and saw her pulling the tiger's tail! Luckily, she was fast and I saw her laughing as she scrambled over the fence like it was no big deal. *Really?!*

I barely had time to catch my breath, and with a groan, I saw her go into another cage. *Please don't be lions*, I thought as I ran to the next spot. I breathed a sigh of relief to see a group of sloths lounging in the trees. Lucky for me, my sister had slowed down as she tried to imitate them. I snuck through the bars and picked my little sister up, and carried her out of the cage. As we were walking back to the zoo exit, I recognized my mom's car.

We got into the car and she said, "Why weren't you answering my texts? Your sister's friend is sick with the flu and couldn't come."

I responded, "Mom! I forgot my phone at the house!"

Then my little sister whined, "I wanted more popcorn, Tim."

I said, "Popcorn is what got us into this mess."

My mom looked confused and asked, "What mess?"

My sister and I looked at each other and both said, "Nothing!"

The Space Between
Meg Gulimlim, age 12

My Trip to the Little League World Series
Riley Gwin, age 12

Last summer, my dad and I went to the Little League World Series in Williamsport, PA. We drove for 18 hours to Cincinnati and got to see a Cincinnati Reds game and we also got to check another stadium off our list. We only stayed there one night because we had to get to Williamsport to meet my friend Conner and his dad. As we were checking into our hotel, we met the Australian team's parents because they were also staying at our hotel. That night, we went to the parade downtown and, as we were watching the teams go by on floats, I was interviewed and was on the evening news!

The next day, we went to the ballpark and watched all four games. We slid down the big hill in centerfield over and over again. We saw the Australian team play that day and after the game, the whole team signed a baseball for us. Then I went to Dick's Sporting Goods and got a new baseball bat. The next morning we went to McDonald's and we met the whole Venezuelan team and took a picture with them.

We were there four days and got to see Pearland and Mo'ne Davis play in two games each. The teams got to stay in a cool looking compound and most of them did not get to see their families very much. I loved going and watching the games. I hope we can go back again next year.

On the Other Side
Marin Hart, age 12

In the year 1942, there lived a girl named Susan Roberts. She was born and raised in Birmingham, England. Susan was about seven years old and had curling brown locks that shone like sparkling copper. She had fair skin and bright, caramel-colored eyes.

Susan also had a great love for her city. She couldn't see the bleary blanket that was war, smothering Birmingham. All she saw were the glistening lights and her beautiful library. The treacherous bombs arrived around two years ago and never left. The town fell into its bleak rhythm.

On the day of July 27, 1942, Susan was off running an errand, as she usually was in the bustling city of Birmingham. Her mother sent her to deliver soup to a friend who had fallen ill and was now staying at the church where she was safest from the bombs. Just a block away from her destination, the air raid siren sounded, sending a chill up her spine. She hurried to the church and stayed there. There were people from all around the area, taking refuge in the church's bomb shelter.

The bombs came, raining down like huge, deadly raindrops. To Susan, it felt like centuries until the ordeal finally ended, but it could not have been more than three hours. When the crashing and booming finally stopped, she sprinted the ten blocks to her home. She thought she must have been going in the wrong direction when she saw only rubble. Tears came to her eyes when the street sign proudly displayed the name of her beloved street. Where had her beautiful neighborhood gone?

Susan trudged up her barren front step to find her home a scattered puzzle. Where were her parents? The thought struck her suddenly. Going against everything her parents had repeated to her again and again, she went to search the rubble. She saw a piece of her grandmother's antique jewelry box and a bit of their kitchen table. Abruptly, she felt a strange pulling sensation. There, in front of her, was a strange ripple in the air. It seemed to allure her closer and closer.

Inspecting it closely, she came forward to poke her finger into the peculiar ripple. Her finger went straight through. Imagining something she had read in her favorite fantasy book, she stepped through.

Dancing colors flew all around her as she was pulled under. She was swirling down what seemed like an endless pit. A moment later, she stopped, her vision clearing. Outside, it looked like Birmingham but not quite *her* Birmingham. She turned back to get out of this odd place, finding only a normal-looking patch of air. The door would never be opened again.

She sat on the nearest stoop and sobbed her heart out. *What have I done?* she asked herself. Susan glanced at a newspaper sitting on the porch of the house. The date read 1923 in bold letters. She felt dizzy and sickened. How did it get to be 1923? She wondered.

A kind woman saw Susan crying on the stoop and said, "What is wrong, little girl?"

"My parents are gone," she sobbed miserably into her hands.

"Why don't we take you to the orphanage and figure things out there?" she soothed.

The little girl, reassured by her kind voice, stood and followed her to the orphanage. She was reticent to tell a soul about the ripple in the sky because she thought they would think she had gone mad! Since that day, Susan lived in that orphanage until the age of twelve, when she was adopted. She grew to dearly love her new parents, but the image of her crumbling, bombed house remained in the back of her mind.

As she got older, she knew the war was approaching. Susan became very passionate about the war effort. She continued to age, but her devotion to this cause never halted.

Her adoptive parents, being fairly wealthy, sent Susan to the Royal Air Force Academy after she desperately pleaded. She trained hard to be a pilot and serve in the war. Susan became almost fanatical about her training. She knew she had to work extra hard to be taken seriously as a young woman.

Her first flight in a small plane was the most exhilarating experience of her life. With map and checklist in hand, an instructor at her side, and excitement in her heart, she took off. A weight lifted off her stomach as the horizon broadened all around them. She soared and flew, the controls feeling utterly natural in her hands. It was the most jubilant she'd felt in a very long time.

She quickly received her pilot's license. Susan was then trained in the nasty business of firing at enemy planes to bring them down. She had to be indifferent to the idea of another person in the plane she had to fire on.

By the year 1942, Susan was twenty-six years old and a skilled fighter pilot. Her dream was to stop the bomb from landing on her beloved childhood home. The dreaded date approached, creeping up on her like something from a nightmare.

Susan woke on the morning of July 27, 1942, for the second time in her life. After eating and dressing, she got in her trusty Avro Lancaster. She started the engine and took off.

She steered her Avro over the spot of the bombing. It was a warm day, the sky the color of lightly shaded pencil lead. Her vision seemed to sharpen, colors becoming more vivid. Susan saw the plane that had changed her fate forever. She looked at her control panel, eyeing the button that would stop the dreaded bomb from falling. She wavered for a moment, the whole world going perfectly still. Then, in one swift moment, she blew up the enemy plane.

There was a huge flash. Whether it was from the bomb or time colliding, she did not know. All that she knew was that young Susan Roberts would never pass through that portal and she would never know of the whole other life she had on the other side.

Skyrim Beginnings
Ellis Haverkamp, age 12

His eyes had just opened. He could barely remember his own name, but he was thankful he did. Then he found himself, Ragonon the Great, in a cart of prisoners. It was foggy and slightly dark as the cart slowly progressed down the dirt road. Ragonon realized that the horse-pulled wagon was being driven by an Imperial.

"Hey, you," the blond Nordic prisoner in front of him said. "You're finally awake. You were trying to cross the border right? Walked right into that Imperial ambush, same as us, and that thief next to me."

It was at that moment that he remembered everything. Just a day ago, Ragonon had been told the final trial to become a Redguard Warrior of Hammerfell. As a Redguard, he was native to Hammerfell and found it right to protect his homeland. The last thing he needed to do was find the most well-fortified bandit fort in all of Hammerfell. The bandits called it, "The Marauder of Hammerfell." The warriors called it a death trap. It was located right on the border from Hammerfell to Skyrim, so that is where he would go. He sheathed his sword, got on his horse, and headed for the border.

But at one moment, he spotted a large group of Nordic warriors. *Stormcloaks?* he thought to himself. As he began to cross paths with them, he spotted a man on a horse, riding at a very high speed.

"Move out of the way!" he shouted. "The Imperials are coming!"

It was too late. He fell to the ground. He raised his head up to see his horse with three arrows in its torso. Ragonon could see that the Imperials and Stormcloaks were in a deep battle. However, he was knocked out too soon to see anything else.

"Curse you, Stormcloaks," the horse thief Ragonon saw during the ambush said. "Skyrim was fine until you came along. The Empire was nice and lazy."

Ragonon noticed it had gotten brighter.

"We are all brothers and sisters in binds now, thief," the Stormcloak said.

"Shut up back there!" the Imperial driver said.

"What's wrong with him, huh?" the thief said to the man next to Ragonon.

Ragonon realized the man had cloth wrapped around his mouth.

"Watch your tongue! You're speaking to Ulfric Stormcloak, the true High King of Skyrim," the Stormcloak said.

If they captured Ulfric, Ragonon knew they weren't going somewhere good. The carts entered Helgen. He could see the leader of the Imperials, General Tullius, along with the elf warriors, the Thalmor. Once they reached the end of the village, the prisoners began to unload. They would tell the Imperials their names and gather around the chopping block. He found that the Stormcloak man's name was Ralof. The thief attempted to run, but the archers were too fast for him, and shot him down.

"Wait. You there. Step forward," the Imperial taking names said to Ragonon. "Who are you?"

He had no other choice. It mattered not anymore. "Ragonon," he replied.

"You don't see many Redguards here anymore. Be you a mercenary?" he asked him.

Ragonon didn't reply.

"Captain, what should we do? He is not on the list," he told the captain.

"Forget the list. He goes to the block," she said.

"By your orders captain."

He was the second one to be called up to the block.

This is the end for Ragonon the Great, he thought. But just as the axe was risen into the air, he saw something. An enormous creature flew off a distant mountain, and came closer, and closer, and closer, until it landed on a tower behind the executioner, who fell to the ground.

"Dragon!" everyone cried.

It let out a ground shaking roar, as the clouds began to form a spiraling shape. Ragonon looked at the ground and held his arms on the back of his head. He was certain this would be his end.

But was that really his name? Were those really his memories? Was he even a man? Who was he? You decide.

Find the true story of the Dragonborn in the Elder Scrolls V: Skyrim.

The Serum
Michael Hoffpauir, age 11

A man in a U.S Army uniform and bag comes running down the hall with two Chinese security guards chasing after him. The man slides under a closing metal door and loses the two guards. He runs to the roof of the building and jumps. The guards get up to the roof just in time to see him in a helicopter taking off.

The pilot says: "Do you have the payload?"

The man in the U.S Army uniform says: "Affirmative."

While the helicopter lands in the loading bay next to three other helicopters, two men walk up to the helicopter. The man in the U.S Army uniform jumps out of the helicopter and walks up to the two men.

The man on the right says: "Major James! Do you have the payload?"

Major James says: "Yes Sir!" He takes off his bag, pulls out a large vial of blue fluid, and hands it to the man on the right. "Here it is, Colonel."

The man on the left says: "Nice job, Major, but we still have to administer it. I would like to show you something, James: Follow me."

James asks the man: "Will you introduce yourself?"

The man says: "Oh my bad. My name is Jack. I work on what I'm about to show you."

They all walk into a small viewing room with a set of windows. On the other side of the windows is a two-story machine.

James says: "What is that?"

With a mesmerized look on his face, Jack says: "This machine is a duplication device."

James says: "So if I have one slice of pizza I could make more?"

"Essentially, yes, but this machine is made for the serum you retrieved. We're not sure what the serum does, so we need to have human testing for it. That's where you come in."

James says: "What!? You're going to use me as your lab rat!?"

"We're not going to force you into it. It's up to you."

James says: "I'll have your answer by tomorrow. Night!"

Jack says: "Night!"

… the next day…

James says: "Come in!"

Jack opens the door and says: "Do you have my answer?"

James says: "I accept."

…10 minutes later…

James and Jack walk into a testing room.

Jack says: "Take a seat. We'll administer the serum in a few short moments."

A man walks through the doorway with a tray and a needle full of serum.

Jack says: "Now stay very still."

They stuck the needle in him and time froze, except James could still move. James tried to figure out what was happening. He pulled out the needle and gestured some hand signs by a simple snap of his fingers. He snapped his fingers and suddenly time unfroze.

Jack says: "The patient is missing!"

James says: "Right behind you! I can control time!"

Jack's mouth hung open.

James and the Colonel are pinned behind sand bags and the Colonel says: "Do it."

James snapped his fingers and everything, but the Colonel and him froze. They ran into a nearby building behind rubble. The Colonel turned the gun on James and pulled his mask off to reveal a Japanese solider, but then the *real* Colonel shot the Japanese solider in the back of the head.

The Colonel says: "We have to end the war for the serum. We have to destroy the serum.

James says: "I agree."

After the war, the serum was destroyed and James went back to serving his country with his newfound powers. Everything went back to normal.

Or did it?

(Machine whirring in background)

The Unexpected Loss
Keierra Hunter, age 12

Today was just a cold, dreary morning and I had just finished my morning entry. After finishing getting dressed, I called August, my boyfriend. All of the sudden, my mom said we were having a family meeting and I could hear in her voice that she was crying. When I got downstairs, I walked to my mom and asked, "What's wrong?"

Shaking nervously, my mom said, "He's dead, He's dead!"

With frustration, I yelled, "WHO?!"

My mom wouldn't answer me and just told me to get in the car. When we got in the car, it was so silent, you could hear katydids bellowing in the wind.

Finally, my mom said, "Your dad was shot by somebody in the Lyons family."

Filled with emotion, I burst into tears with a thousand thoughts racing through my mind. All I could think was why did they do this? Who did this, and when did they do this?

After a while, we drove to the morgue to identify my dad's body. When we got in the driveway of the morgue, my mom and I decided to pray. After we finished praying, we went inside and told the people who we were and they said go to room 235. When we got there, I stopped at the door to breathe because I knew that as soon as I walked in there, I was going to go crazy with tears. I think my mom saw I was scared so she held my hand and walked in with me. When we got there and saw the body lying there motionless, my mom went crazy. The doctor came and escorted her out to tell her how he died and to try to calm her down as best as he could. While they were outside, I walked up to the body and saw my dad, my flesh, my blood. When my mom came in, I told her that dad was shot by Luscious Lyons. She asked me how I knew and I showed her his signature mark. After we were done viewing the body, we went home and my mom said she was going to be in her room sleeping. I told her I was going to August's house, but

I wasn't, I was going to the Lyons house. When I arrived, I knocked on the door and the security guard opened it and checked me to make sure I didn't have a gun. After he was done, he walked me to the family room where everyone was.

"Hello everybody; I hope I'm not intruding," I said.

Luscious replied "No, but you were not invited to this family meeting, probably because you're not family."

I answered him with frustration. "No, but my dad was a part of this family, but I guess not anymore, since he's dead!"

Cookie cut in. "Honey, what are you talking about? Who killed your dad?"

I said to her with so much anger, "Ask your ex-husband. I'm pretty sure he knows. Don't you Luscious?"

Luscious lied right to my face, "No, I have no idea what you're talking about."

"Really Luscious, you're going to tell me that you didn't kill my dad," I said. I pulled out the picture of my dad laying on the examination table

"I didn't do anything to your dad," he said.

"Ok so I'm crazy, alright. I apologize for intruding;" I said and with that, I left.

When I got into the car, I started crying.

It has been a year since my dad's death, and I can still hear him call my name in the middle of the night. Luscious Lyons, the man that killed my dad, is in jail for life and I'm ok with that. I do still wish my dad were here to know that I graduated early as valedictorian of my high school. My mom and I are still trying to live with the hurt and pain of my dad's death. For me, I pray every day and wish that my dad comes back, but deep down, I know that he's in a better place. When I woke up, I told my mom I was going to the cemetery to talk to my dad and visit his tombstone. As I left, she told me to be back before one o'clock for lunch. When I arrived at the cemetery, I went and sat on the ground and started talking.

"Hi, daddy. I'm doing well and so is mom. I'm still sad that you died, but I've accepted that you are gone by knowing you're in a better place. Sometimes I wish that you could come back, like when I graduated as valedictorian. Since singing was your thing, I decided to take singing classes and so far, I'm doing well at it. I've also started filling out applications for college. UCLA is the college I plan to attend because that was your college. I will talk to you again sometime soon, but right now, I have to get going because Mom and I have a lunch date."

With that, I got off the ground, dusted off my butt, and got in the car to drive home. When I got home, my mom was sitting on the couch ready to go, and we decided to go to Red Lobster to eat lunch. My mom said she had a surprise for me and pulled out a big envelope from UCLA. I grabbed it really fast and opened it. When I read it, all I saw was, "Congratulations, you have been accepted to UCLA. See you in the fall." I screamed and started to thank God and my dad.

When we got home, I called August and told him the good news and he told me he was accepted too. Later that day, I went back to the cemetery and told my dad what happened. When I was done talking to him, I went home, prayed, and went to sleep.

Stuffed Drama
Ashlei Johnson, age 12

In Dalla, Texas, there is a store that has everything you've ever dreamed of, like phones, tablets, toys, clothes, food, and many other items that will draw your attention. As I strolled through the aisles of the grand store, I passed a shelf with a sign that read, "Rainbow Loom." I gazed down the shelves in excitement. I nearly lost my breath at the sight of rubber bands. Well, since almost every kid in school had rubber bands and used them to make bracelets, necklaces, and even rings, I thought about how nice it would be to have everybody begging for rubber bands from me. As my mom and I gazed all the way to the price tags, she decided that I'd be better off making my own rubber bands.

Well, since rubber bands were thirteen dollars for a pack of 100, I didn't know what to do, but I knew that those rubber bands would leave with me. I thought of many ways, like politely asking the cashier or manager, but I knew that wouldn't work. Next, I thought of begging my mom for the rubber bands until she couldn't take it anymore, even though I had already tried and it did not work. Finally, I had no other choice but to steal the overpriced rubber bands. I know you're wondering how I would steal packs of rubber bands, and honestly, I didn't know how to steal them either. After twenty-seven aisles of thinking, I finally came up with a plan. I was going to wait until the aisle was completely empty and quietly sneak into the aisle, snatch a lot of packs, and stuff them into my purse. Then, I'd gracefully walk back to my mother like nothing happened. Now, the time had come. The time for me to commit my very first crime. I quietly took deep breaths, then maneuvered my way through the crowded aisle without my mother knowing. I tip toed to aisle number seven, the rainbow loom aisle. In a flash of lightning, I took seven packs of rubber bands. Then, the announcement speaker came on. It was my mom. She was looking for me. I ran all the way to the counter where my mom was. She looked worried. Since she had already checked out, I was happy to walk out with ease. Then, I saw two of my worst nightmares, two huge security guards. They were checking everybody's bags and purses. I became nervous. So, I hid my purse to the side and, to my surprise, they didn't see it. I walked out of the store with a slight grin. Then, as I turned around, a security guard was running for my bag. Mom quickly made us stop, and told me to let him check my purse. He found several packs of rubber bands and became furious.

He asked us to make our way to the security counter. As I approached the counter, the security guard asked for my purse so he could see if there was anything else. Mom looked at me with disappointment and I felt ashamed. The security guards took a photo of me and put it in the records of crime. Well, that didn't go as planned, but at least I got the rubber bands because I was the youngest person to ever commit a crime at the store. Mom wouldn't let me have them until I apologized sincerely to the guards and completely cleaned my room. Now I know not to ever take things that don't belong to me, especially at a store.

Stealing is not the answer to your problems. Save up your allowance and pay for them yourself!

Nacomi and Moni-Pack Wolves
Jolie Jones, age 12

One day in the Alaskan woods, trouble started. The alpha male, Scar, was very angry at the pack. His youngest pup, Nacomi, was missing. His mate, Phara, asked the wolf pack where she was.

Moni, a friend of Nacomi said, "Nacomi is going to live in a rival wolf clan."

Scar was furious and demanded, "Everyone must stop and find my daughter!"

Nacomi was playing in a nearby meadow. Being a young pup of only 3 years, she was unaware of the danger that faced her. Nearby eyes watched her every move. It was the rival wolf clan's youngest son, Hunter. He was about her same age. Nacomi saw him and darted off. Hunter ran after her.

Nacomi ran to her father, "Daddy he is chasing me!"

Scar said, "Who dear?"

She said, "Another wolf is chasing me!"

Hunter came up on the two and said, "She is mine!"

Scar said, "Never!"

Then Hunter said, "She must come and live with my pack!"

Nacomi cried, "Say no Dad, Mom please!"

Phara, the alpha female said, "I'm sorry daughter!"

Hunter said, "Tonight!" And he darted off.

Nacomi ran and laid down under a tree near the pack.

Moni, Nacomi's friend said, "Me and the wolf pack are so sorry!"

Nacomi said, "It's ok!"

That night, Nacomi put a flower in her glistening white fur. She went to the rival wolf clan with her pack. She alone went up to the top of the rock and met Hunter.

He said, "Hey you look nice!"

Nacomi said, "Thanks."

They howled all night. Then, when Hunter wasn't looking, Nacomi ran to Moni and said, "Let's run away!" So, Nacomi and Moni ran miles and miles and found a family.

The family thought they were dogs and fed them meat. The family saw there was no collar on either wolf.

Their kids said, "Can we have them?" The kids hugged the wolves.

The parents said, "OK!"

So, they let the wolves into the car and drove off. The wolves lived on and never saw the wolf pack again.

Blue Tears
Tori Jones, age 12

"Look, look at her
Over there crying"
Say the cool kids
But they don't know I'm dying

When I walk through the hall
All the children stare
I don't dare make eye contact
Just wish I had hair

I talk to my friends
The ones no one sees
All I do is complain
About my horrid disease

I put tissue in my shirt
I push out tight
But then I look down
Left is still bigger than right

Every night I cry
A deep cry off fear
That I might die the next day
So I cry a blue tear

Forever in my Dreams

Viviana Juarez, age 11

Have you ever asked yourself how it would feel to get stuck in your own dream? Well I have and it all changed that one Friday night. All I could think of was my first date tomorrow. I am really nervous; I don't know what to say when I meet her. All I want is to have a nice day and dream about the positives and the negatives. As I was thinking about my date, my parents came in to kiss me goodnight. My mom closed the door and all I could think was *what if something goes wrong on my first date.* Thinking about all the negatives made me finally fall asleep with the noise of the owls, the movement of the trees, and sound of the ocean waves. As I closed my eyes, I heard a click and saw a bright light. I didn't recognize the place until I saw a yellow car with flowers. The second I saw the car, I knew it was my date's car. All of a sudden, I was wearing a tuxedo and walking to the front door.

The girl asked me if I was ready for our first date and I coolly said, 'Yes!"

We had reservations at a fancy Italian restaurant and when I opened the door, it hit me in the head. I knew that the date would end badly. Being a gentleman, I pulled out her chair and she took a seat. As we started talking, I realized I enjoyed our conversation, but then I spilled her drink all over us. We rushed to the restroom to clean off the drink, but something told me it was a dream and I was stationary in the dream. We were both ready to leave and go back to the house. On the way, we passed a green light, yellow light, and a red light. Something made me accelerate when I came to the red light. From the side I could see a fast approaching car.

The next thing I knew, I was at the hospital with my parents. They told me I wouldn't wake up and they were worried that something bad happened to me in my sleep. I told them I did and I was forever in my dreams.

Sam: An Alien Student

Kaz Kelly, age 11

Sam is an alien that lives on planet Blaar Blaar. He was just like you and I, having to go to a dreaded place called "school." He was just a normal kid in the 6th grade and he walked to school and back every day. He kept this routine since the first day of school, but on one particular day, something strange happened...

A METEORITE CRASHED ON PLANET BLAAR BLAAR!!!

What were you thinking? A bad guy takes Sam?! What's wrong with you?!

Well, anyway, what I was saying, the meteorite crashed onto the planet causing the whole planet to act radioactive.

Wait, what did I say?! I didn't say anything...

(Gulp) "Hey Rick, we weren't supposed to save that until the end of the story!"
(Cough)

Umm ... Well, when Sam got home, he sat down to watch TV and on the news, the anchor said to "Stay indoors at all costs." So Sam tried to tell his parents that he needed to stay home the next day, but his parents said, "No," so he had to go to school the next day. So, he decided to just get a good night's sleep. The next day, he mysteriously woke up AT THE SCHOOL. It was like a paranormal experience. There weren't many kids at the school, but surprisingly enough, none of the teachers were absent.

"Wow, they really must need the money." Sam said in alien language. *That's it*, He thought. *I am getting out of here!*

So when the teacher walked outside of the classroom, he ran out, making sure none of the teachers, security, or custodians saw him.

When he escaped the school, something strange happened. It felt like something hit his back, he fell into a deep sleep, and then when he woke up. He was surprised.

"Oh my Blaar ...," Sam said.

To be continued . . .

Just turn the page!

Is it not obvious?!

Sam: An Alien Student Part 2

The whole neighborhood was... was... junglefied! To his surprise, Sam looked back and the school wasn't there. Now is when he realized something REAL is going on!!! He wanted to see if his home was still there because some houses were still visible through the vines (Obviously, the vines were covering everything!). He thought there was some sort of portal or something near his house. The journey itself was crazy. Sam had to swing across the vines, climb on moss, and anything you thought was impossible.

Of course, as soon as he approached his house, a weird, gross, huge piranha plant came out of the vines and ate Sam!

Sure, I know what you're thinking, "Oh, he died?"

Nope.

Sam woke up the next day, in the same spot he did last time. This time, the neighborhood was all cute, fuzzy flowers and stuff.

Uhh ... What happened?! he thought.

It worked just like last time, only everything was covered in grass and dirt! He navigated bees from flower to flower, walked the "Yellow Brick Road," and so on and so forth. But this time, he was eaten by... uhh... a bunny. Yeah, a bunny.

Then he woke up in the same generic spot, but this time, everything was normal, other than the fact that he was the size of an ant. He walked the path he usually took from school to his house, but halfway there, a car turned on to the sidewalk and crushed him! But this time, he didn't wake up in front of the school, he woke up in his bed! He looked around just to check if everything was normal. Sam got out of his bed and walked into the living room just to find out it was four in the morning. He went back to sleep so he wouldn't upset his parents.

"It was all a dream. . ."

The End

Untitled
Francesca Khurana, age 13

I yelled,

And pushed myself in the darkness of the closet.

I stuck myself inside.

I like the dark,

It was like my friend.

Sitting knees in,

Face down,

Tears falling,

Imagination closed,

Mind blank,

Except…

Him.

He overcame me.

Writing,

Writing,

Writing.

Tears,

Tears,

Tears.

One thing he said to me,

Made me a thousand more.

My fear was losing him,

But I never thought I already lost him.

He still possesses me,

Even though,

It is a broken dream now.

It is like hearing a song,

That finishes,

Without hearing the last word,

Incomplete.

Three red roses for you,

To remember me.

Seasons
Destiny Lara, age 14

We all bloom

Some bloom fine

Others with sickness

Though all the same

Surviving until the winters fall

Come alive in the spring

Struggle through the heat of the summer

Calm with the autumn

And wither in the winter

How Can You Love to Suffer
Destiny Lara, age 14

Falling apart is not beautiful

Or a joke

There is nothing lovely

About my scars

Or the way my friend was addicted to snow

Just to forget his sadness

His protruding bones

Nor her sleepless nights

Are enchanting

How can you find romance in

Their purple, blue, stinging skin

Being told "I'm the only one who loves you"

And non-consensual actions

Waking from a nightmare

Crying, shaking

Is not cute

Uncontrollable shifts in mood

Turns lights on and off 20, 21, 22, 23, 24 times
Unable to stay still as the mind races
Are no joke

There is nothing charming
About suffering

Tesoro
Destiny Lara, age 14

I want you to get out of my thoughts

And into my arms

Is your home

A person

Or a place

I've been homeless

But now I'm not home

I love you with all my heart

Don't ever forget that

I won't love anyone more than you

I just wanna hold you right now

I love you, I love you

I miss you

You 're the brightest thing in my life

Your Star
Destiny Lara, age 14

I wish my best friend never scarred his wings

I wish my friend never danced with the lady in white

I wish my friend could feel the love

And oh if could

I would take their pains

And agony

To keep them myself

Even if it drives me insane,

It doesn't matter

At least they would find

Happiness and

Comfort

I would face the harsh winter storm

I fit meant they

Only felt the spring's warmth

1/29/15
Destiny Lara, age 14

Even though the cold skies

Might reflect what's inside

I came to realize

Killing yourself is no way

To rid of your sadness

It will just continue living in the souls of others

Your smile may not be the

Sunshine

But it's bright like the Moon light

There is light

In the darkest places of your heart

And roses in your mind

Goodnight
Destiny Lara, age 14

I WILL NOT LET MY EYES BE DARK

LIKE MY MIND

OR MY HAIR MESSY

LIKE MY THOUGHTS

I CANNOT BELIEVE

IT TOOK ME THIS LONG TO REALIZE

NOTHING IS WRONG

BUT I SURE CAN'T STOP FEELING LIKE

EVERYTHING IS OUT OF PLACE

NOW THAT THE HURRICANE IS GONE

AND THE DUST HAS ALMOST CLEARED

I'M ONLY DIFFERENT

BECAUSE I UNDERSTAND THINGS

THAT THEY DON'T

I SHOULD NOT BE SHAMED FOR THAT

MY DREAMS ARE TOO BIG

FOR THIS CITY TO HANDLE

LIFE IS MOVING ON AND SO SHOULD I

SURE I AM SCARED AND ALONE

BUT I'M FINE

THERE ARE SOME DAYS WHERE

I AM KAHLO

AND OTHERS I AM GOGH

BUT THAT'S OK

BECAUSE I AM HUMAN

AND I CAN NOT CONTROL MY EMOTIONS

I MAY NOT HAVE THE SUN IN MY EYES

OR LOVE FLOWING THROUGH MY VEINS

NOT EVEN A BEAUTIFUL NEBULA IN MY MIND

BUT RATHER LIGHT RAIN IN MY MIND

HAVE YOU EVER DANCED IN THE RAIN?

AND FIRE RUNNING THROUGH MY VEINS

HAVE YOU EVER SAT BY A FIRE WITH A FRIEND?

THAT'S OK, I HAVEN'T EITHER

AND THERE'S DIRT IN MY EYES

BECAUSE EVERY FLOWER

HAS TO GROW THROUGH DIRT

Ultimate Battle Aliens vs. Humans
Agustin Mejia, age 11

BOOM! went an asteroid on an alien planet. Only a few aliens survived. They took the biggest ship on their planet and took as many aliens as they could. The ship was so large, they began a new life in it until they could find a new planet to live on. Back on Earth things where peaceful, and there was a man who had been in wars before. That man had a three year old son named John, and John always liked to play fight with his father. He sometimes got in fights at school. When John turned 11, the aliens arrived on Earth, but they were so rude that they did not want to share the planet with the humans. They started to kill humans at night, but when the humans found out, they got one man from every family for a war. You had to at least be eighteen years old to be in the war. The war took place all over the world and sadly, the aliens won the war.

The humans evacuated the Earth, but John did not want to. John formed his own team, stayed on Earth secretly, and killed aliens alongside his group. The aliens found them one day and the leader sent a small group to kill them. Sadly, one of John's teammates died. They went to their base which is an abandoned laboratory. All the teammates had a specialty which was their job. John worked with a girl named Gwen. He had a crush on her, and she had a crush on him. Their job was engineering and they had been working on an old military jet plane, but they mostly worked on weapons and ammo. Another teammate was Spike. His specialty was muscle so he guarded the base. Jason, the one who died in battle, was supposed to do graphing and calculations, because his specialty was intelligence. They searched around the base one day and found a device that had a round part like a dish but was much larger. They searched it up on a computer, and it was a device that could send a signal to any vehicle called a signal beam. That got them thinking: What if they sent a signal to the plane the people left on? Maybe they would come back. So they went ahead, and sent the signal to the ship. They waited a few years, but the ship never came.

One day, the aliens found their base. Spike told John and Gwen that they were coming and to run. Gwen did not want to go because Spike was her brother. Spike told John to take good care of her, and take her away from here.

"Do not turn back," said Spike, and off went Gwen and John.

The alien lord was expecting that they would go different ways, so he set up a trap. Gwen and John fought together like they were meant to. They tried to beat the aliens but their team work was not enough and they were captured.

The lord of the aliens said to John, "Since you love your precious planet. We can make a deal, we share the planet if you marry my daughter Melisa."

Although John knew that he had his heart set on someone else. John asked if there was another way, but the alien lord responded, "No."

If John refused, he and Gwen would perish there. Gwen looked at John with a sad face like if she was telling him not to do it. John knew the right thing to do, and he said no. They fought again, and they were doing well until Melisa went up against Gwen and she was too strong. John stepped in and finished Melisa off. The alien lord got so furious that he threw Gwen to the side, and went after John while he was fighting other aliens. The alien lord knocked John down to the floor, and right when the lord was about to end John, a spike came out of nowhere and slashed the alien lord's head off.

Then more alien soldiers came. The team fought a lot of them, but then came the real end of Spike. Gwen fought fiercely, but they ran out of ammo.

John said to Gwen, "If this is the end, I need to tell you something."

Gwen answered, "Yes?"

While fighting, he said, "I love you."

Then, all the sudden, the space ship came back and all the people fought for their home planet. On that very day, they killed every last alien on Earth. They went back to living peacefully.

After the whole war, Gwen asked John, "What where you saying

about you loving something or someone?"
　　Then a few years later they got married.

New Year
Madison Montgomery, age 12

We opened the bottles of sparkling cider. We put 12 grapes in each bag for my brother, my in-laws, and me. We watch them count down 30, 29, 28, 27, 26, 25, 24, 23, 22, 21, 20... We all grabbed the grapes and stuffed them in our mouths. My in-law, Eddie, won and made his wish. I thought we all looked funny stuffing all those grapes in our mouths. Then the crowds went 5, 4, 3, 2, 1. We all went outside to watch fireworks, blew our noise makers, and we took a family photo.

I was happy to be home in Farmington with my in-laws and family. When snow was falling, I felt happy. When I was with my future in-laws and family I was happy. Nothing was better than being in Farmington with my family on New Year. Nothing could ruin my special day and nothing could ruin my special moment. Not today, not tomorrow, not ever in all my life. What could go wrong? Nothing at all. Life is good here.

I was in my beautiful home with the snow falling on the hills and mountains. I bet over those hills and mountains, more of my family watched the beauty of New Year with us. All of the beautiful colors in the air and the nicest people are here in life. My life is good here in Farmington tonight. The beauty is here and all things special in life. When I was stuffing all those grapes in my mouth with my family, I was happy I was here doing it with them. When the New Year came, I was happy that I spent it with the people I love most in my special life.

Circus Mania
Leslie Morales, age 12

I slowly opened up my eyes. Not knowing what was happening at the moment, I took a look at what was around me. It seemed I was in a cage. Without noticing, I spoke out loud, "Wh-where am I?" A moment of silence fell upon me.

"Oh, so you're awake, newbie."

I gazed over to where the high-pitched voice was coming from. What I found was a woman, around her 20's or so. She had raggedy old clothes, her skin was white as snow, and from her scent and all the dirt on her body, you could tell she had not taken a bath in a long time. I crawled to the edge of the cage that was closest to the strange woman.

"Where am I? Why am I here? Who am I?"

As soon as I finished speaking, she examined me with her ice-cold eyes from where she was sitting. "You'll know once it's your turn."

When she finished her sentence, the area where she was sitting rose up and the only thing I could hear were screams and laughter. This was so truly terrifying that I didn't even know how to react. My time of being slightly terrified was over after I felt that I was being dragged. Before, I was feeling slightly terrified. Now, I feel like I'm actually going to die in this place. I was roughly thrown on a table and tied down with ropes. They were smelly and itchy, so I had a big urge to get them off me. As I squirmed around on the table, trying to escape, a person who seemed to be the boss came in and approached me with a grey, small, shiny collar in his hand. He was old, smelly as skunk spray, and was so buff it looked like he lifted weights all day long, non-stop.

"Hello there. I'm going to be your new boss for pretty much the rest of your life."

A little giggle came out of my mouth. His voice was high-pitched just like a little girl's. Anyone would laugh at that, right? He kept walking towards me and when he was just inches away, he roughly whispered in my ear, "Don't worry about this thing I'm going to put you on. It won't hurt. Much. Or so I think."

Without warning, he snapped the collar on my neck. It was the worst feeling ever. It felt as if electricity was roughly running through my body. The pain faded away slowly and it seemed as if nothing happened at all. Again, without warning, I was dragged into a place where millions of people were staring at me. In front of me was a cage, and inside of it was a mechanical lion, or so I thought. Next to me was a sword and an axe. I grabbed the sword and axe and suddenly heard a roaring sound. The mechanical lion was finally released and, of course, it was headed towards me. I followed my instincts and swung the sword around. The lion just roared at me and was slowly approaching. *What is going on? Am I even doing this?* I had many questions that I wanted answered but right now, I had to somehow survive this human-eating-mechanical-beast thing. The people watching me were booing and throwing tomatoes at the cage that I was in. With that, I easily concluded that I was part of a "do-or-die" type of show. I kept swinging the sword in front of the creature, and somehow, I was able to cut its head off. Green goo was dripping from where the head was supposed to be. My mind couldn't take this and I was about to vomit.

I quickly ran back and suddenly bumped into a girl. "Ouch! Watch where you're going, newbie!" I recognized that voice. It was the girl from before!

I quickly stood up and helped her get up "S-sorry. I didn't see you."

"Yeah, I can tell. So how was your first show?" She paused for a moment, looked at the collar I had on, and then spoke again "...Smile?"

I was confused. "Who's Smile?"

"That's your stage name. It says so in the collar you have on. Look, mine is Tear." She tapped her collar and it said Tear. "Well, we should get going."

Our lives in this weird world full of circus based deadly traps went on. I got better at doing acts; I made lots of friends, and so on.

It was fine until one day that friend of mine, Scar, rushed to me as he screamed my name as loud as he could.

"Calm down. Did something happen?"

"Yes! Tear is fighting the mechanical beast, and you know how weak she is. She couldn't take it and so she got attacked roughly. Right now, she's in the private hospital."

I didn't even have to think twice. I ran as fast as I could to the room where the best friend I've had since I joined this show was horribly injured. I swung the door opened and slid into a chair beside her. I firmly held her hand and tears fell on our hands. She was covered in blood-soak bandages and very painful stitches.

I whispered very quietly so that no one would hear me, "Why did you do something so dangerous?"

An unexpected response came upon me… "Didn't you do something like this too?"

The Death of Evil
Trinity Mosier, age 12

They say Hitler killed himself. However, this statement is incorrect.

BOOM! BOOM! BOOM! "WE ARE THE NAZIS!" voices shouted from behind the door. "WE HAVE COME TO ARREST YOU! OPEN THE DOOR IMMEDIATELY!" they yelled again.

"They're here. They've found us," Mama whispered.

"Amalia, take Lorelei and hide!" Papa said.

"But they'll kill you!" I said. "They'll take you to one of those camps for Jewish people and finish you off!"

He replied, "That doesn't matter. What matters is you! Now go, before they find you!"

I grabbed her hand, and we ran all the way to the back of the house. There was a washing machine about three yards away from the back door. Lorelei and I huddled together.

"Are there any more of you?" the Nazis asked.

We heard Mama's feeble reply, "No, we are the only ones who live here."

"If you're lying, we will soon know, since we will be searching your house," a different voice said.

That was my cue. Knowing what would happen if we stayed where we were, I told Lorelei softly, "We need to go now, baby." Helping her up, I hurried to the back door, holding her hand.

Once outside, I explained to her that we had to run away. The only thought that was coursing through my mind was *We have to get out of Bremerhaven and head towards Berlin.* We started running and didn't stop, even when one of the Nazis tried to halt us. He started chasing us, but we easily outran him. Eventually, we made it to the train station.

"Two tickets to Berlin, please!" I told the man behind the counter.

Berlin is where Hitler's base is, and where he is at the moment. I knew that the Nazis were going to kill Mama and Papa. Devising a plan of revenge for them was easy; I was going to kill Adolf Hitler. I had not yet explained this to Lorelei, and I did not know how I was going to.

We boarded the train, and when seated, I asked Lorelei, "Do you know what is going to happen to Mama and Papa?"

She replied, "I think so. Are those men that came in our house going to kill them?"

I did not reply, but I think we both knew the answer. I thought to myself, *She's really smart, being only five.* We sat unspeaking for a while, and then I explained to her that we were going to Berlin where I was going to kill the man who killed our parents. We sat in silence until both of us fell asleep. When I awoke, I saw the twinkling city lights of Berlin against the black midnight sky.

"Lorelei!" I whispered. "Lorelai, wake up! We're in Berlin!" I said.

Lorelai, dazed and confused, looked out the window with eyes as wide as dinner plates.

"It's *beautiful.*" She replied.

Once off the train, I purchased a map and found the location of Hitler's base. Finding a way to get there, however, was trickier, since I knew the Nazis would be after us by now. I thought to myself that walking was too risky, they would be controlling the buses. Eventually, we decided that we were going to take a taxi to our destination. During the ride, I thought of how I was going to kill Hitler. Finally, I heard a voice.

"Amalia… AMALIA!!!" Lorelei shouted in my ear. "We're here," she said.

We thought Hitler was in his bunker below the building, and there did not seem to be any staircases in this room. We searched the whole building and surprisingly did not run into *any* Nazis. What we saw amazed us because around the corner was Hitler. Suddenly, I noticed his gun on the table in front of him. Silent as a fox, I snatched the gun and raised it, aiming for his head. As my finger curled around the trigger, I thought, *Come on. This is the moment you've been waiting for.* The gun surprisingly fired and, in slow motion, he turned around as the bullet penetrated his skull. As he fell, his last words were, "You are Jewish."

As his dead body hit the ground, the building started collapsing. I ran all the way out, and I thought my sister was behind me, but when I looked back, she was gone.

"Lorelai!" I shouted. "Lorelai!" My voice started to break. "Lorelai, where are you?" I said again with fear.

I couldn't hold back my tears. Running back to the wreckage, I saw her there, barely alive. I held her, saying, "Don't cry. Don't cry."

She looked up at me and said, "You were a good sister, Amalia. I wish I could've lived longer and seen the world, but now that I will not see it, you do it. Do that for me." Then, she died in my arms.

I started to cry even harder than before. "I killed him, but I lost you." I said to her. "It should've been me who died."

I began to think, *The loss of my sister was too high of a price to pay for the revenge that I got. I would bring Hitler back from the dead if Lorelei could come back too.*

Dragons of the East and West
Carolyn Ngo, age 13

The Granny Escapade
Abigail Nitsch, age 11

Running fast with my heart pounding, I was finally free from the sight of jail. Sorry, I mean my nursing home. I'm sure you're wondering why me, a grandma that is supposed to be in a wheelchair, is running. Well, I'm not your ordinary granny, I'm Ninja Granny. You are also probably wondering if any family would be mourning over my death if I failed my mission. Yes, my granddaughter, Jenny, would be sad, but my husband, mother, father, and siblings were all killed in a mission-gone-wrong when she was nine. I can probably guess her thoughts now that jail has most likely notified her.

What if she's fallen into the bayou? What if she's fallen and can't get up? What if she's been kidnapped? No, stop worrying, because she should be fine.

Usually the Ninja Agency would call in another ninja, but they've been trying to get these guys for weeks. The other ninjas were all injured, so they had to call me in. That was the first time they've done so since I've been incognito in the nursing home. I looked at my ninja watch, and discovered I was two miles away from the enemy. I disguised myself as an innocent old lady, instead of having my nursing gown on, and ran towards the bad guys. When I approached the targets, I asked them where the perfume shop was located. As I punched one of them in the face while saying thank you, I threw him into the other person.

"Bye, bye little spies." That was too easy.

Just then, I heard movement behind me. A bag was thrown over my head and I was dragged into the alley to the right of me. I had spoken too soon because I had been kidnapped and was off to meet the "Big Guys." I was forced into a chair and told to stay—as if I could go anywhere with a bag over my head. They asked me who I was and I said, "Audrey Ann." They asked me why I beat up the two guys. I said, "Because they gave me the wrong directions to the perfume shop." After a few more questions, they said that they would take the bag off of my head very slowly and asked me not to do anything stupid. When they took it off, I jumped up and started fighting all five of them because that wasn't stupid. It was smart. Three boys, two girls... easy enough. I did a backflip while kicking one boy and one girl in the face. Someone came after me, so I kicked her down. I knocked another guy out, leaving me with one boy. We both sized each other up and attacked. I fought him for a good five minutes before I got him down and sat on his head.

All in a day's work, I thought as I brushed off my shoulders, walked to where I had stowed my wheelchair, and put my nursing home gown back on. I got in my wheelchair and roamed the streets for cops to see me and take me back to jail.

When they found me, I acted innocent and said that I didn't even know that I had left the nursing home and thought that I was just rolling down the hallway. When I saw Jenny, I pulled her aside and said, "I am getting old, so I need to tell you that you have been born into a family of ninjas and have been accepted into a school to train..."

Not Just a Dog
Olivia Nixon, age 12

Every once in a lifetime someone or something changes someone's whole life. For me, this person turned my whole life upside-down, backwards, sideways, any way it could be changed. Yeah, yeah, I know, everyone has someone who impacted their life greatly, but my person is just a little bit different.

"How?" you ask.

Well, the person who impacted my life is actually a dog.

About a year ago, at the beginning of 5th grade, my family and I decided we wanted to get another dog. About a month after that decision, before we knew it, we were driving in our beige, GMC Yukon to the person who was selling the dog. The excitement only built, questions like "How many more minutes?!" and "What's her name going to be?" only became more common. We walked in and there she was, a chubby little English bulldog puppy, didn't look like much, but little did I know that dog would change my whole perspective on life.

I was bullied severely in elementary school. Most days I would go home crying, tears rolling down my face. I didn't really have that many friends, maybe 3 or 4, but they were in a different class. No one really liked me much, but our new dog did. This was pretty shocking to me, pets normally liked my brother most. But this dog followed me everywhere around the house. She was always by my side. I thought only joy could come from this dog, but I would soon find out that my life would come crashing down because of her.

We named her Lexington, Lexi for short. One day, she had to go to the vet to get spaded and when she got back from her veterinarian appointment she just wasn't herself. She wouldn't get up to eat, she wouldn't even walk. Lexi just sat at the end of the bed not moving a muscle. You could tell she was in pain. At about 9:00 pm we started to get very worried and decided we had to take her to a hospital. I mean, she had sat in the same spot for the past 2 days. It was too late for me and my sister to go to the animal emergency hospital so my mom and brother went instead, but I had a feeling it was too late for Lexi as well. For my sister and I, we just waited and waited, then waited some more to hear from my mother what is happening. The phone rang. It was my mom, I suddenly felt my heart just shatter and tears silently rolled down my face. A minute later, my dad called me and my sister downstairs.

I walked into my parents' bedroom. My dad was sitting there as quiet as can be. We were all silent for a moment. I broke the silence and with the warm tears flowing down my face, said, "She's dead isn't she?"

My dad nodded silently.

My best friend was dead, but in a way, she wasn't. No matter how much it hurt I will always have the memories.

That dog taught me so much; she taught me that no matter how sucky things get, that they will get better. She taught me that life is short and I shouldn't be wasting my time on the ones I hate, but instead spending it with the ones I love. If I listed everything she taught me, we would be here for hours. She was barely nine months old, but she had taught me more than people way older who get paid to teach as a living.

That dog made me into the person I am today. I stopped caring what the bullies thought about me, or care about what they said to me, because all of that didn't matter. I knew it wasn't true and so did my family and close friends and that is what mattered. I started to come home with a smile on my face instead of tears. I am a much better, more positive person than I was a year ago and I have that very dog, Lexington, to thank for all of that.

I still miss her and I certainly will never forget her.

Shoes I Don't Really Wear
Daniel Nunes, age 13

Skate Life
Edwin Panameno, age 14

Galavanting Goat
Maya Parani, age12

As the wind rustles my mountain goat hair, I squint into the sunset... I am just a goat and I managed to climb this gargantuan rock of glory. The sharp edges of the glistening structure grace my hooves. Good thing I am not going downhill. Suddenly, I hear a faint "BAAR" as I gaze into the distance. The silhouette of a magnificent goat shines in the subtle light of the descending sun. My heart beats to the sound of her hooves clicking against the hard, rocky mountain. Unfortunately, she is on another mountain across the field, not on my mountain. I have to talk to her! But what will I say? "BAAAH"...

I won't have to say anything if I give her a present, so I'll do just that! I scan the rocky terrain and spot the perfect gift, a mouthwatering, luscious, delicious, thorn barbed vine. There were roses on top, too, but everybody knows that goats love thorns. I stuff them in my mouth, and without thinking, I sprint off the pinnacle.

I stumble on a huge boulder and start rolling down the summit with the thorns gently cradled in my mouth. As I rotate, grime splatters against my handsome face... *I hope she likes the outdoorsy type?*

As I strike the soft musky surface, I notice the rushing river. I study the river as I rise. Knowing I can't swim, I make the decision to cross. Tap dancing pebble to stone to rock, I hold my breath as I near the far bank.

Approaching the safety of the dry land, a hungry wolf jolts out of the high grass. I leap and do a double summersault, bounce off of the beast's snapping jaw, and kick off for a three point landing ashore. The stunned wolf loses his footing and sails down the river. I quicken my pace and continue my journey towards the hill of my romantic future.

Thinking I am clear of danger, I suddenly hear a *SWOOSH!* As the thorns get snatched out of my mouth, I spot a small brown curious monkey swinging away from me. Panicked, I chase the monkey trying to reach his tail. The monkey starts laughing hysterically as I continue chasing his foolishness. In a very un-goatlike manner, I jump and grab his active tail. Shocked by my sudden athletic ability, the monkey releases the prize and scrambles for the high treetops. I catch my thorns and I can finally breathe a sigh of relief.

Back to the original mission: angel goat awaits me. With a renewed focus, I head up towards my field of dreams.

I reach the clearing where I last saw that stunning ewe. I notice I am alone...no one to be seen at all, not even a squirrel. With the soggy, wet, monkey breath thorns still in my mouth, I look back across the field to the mountain, the gargantuan rock of glory, and what do I see? It's my dream goat standing alone in the same clearing that I just left. We stare at each other in mutual disappointment. If only I could tell her about my heroic adventure...

For now, the only thing I can think of is that I just "goat" to go out there and get her.

She's my dream goat, the queen of all goats.

Dare to Dream
Elizabeth Parker, age 12

Antonio the Drifter
Eryn Perez Limon, age 14

Darkness and Tunnel
Laura Phelps, age 14

Life has corruptions you're in a tunnel
It's a new day push them away
You see no light shine through
You feel alone
There may be darkness around you
There's always light at the end
Of the tunnel just hold on
Even if you're at the end of your tail

Don't look at life as hell
You're here for a reason
There's a pulse a beat in your wrist
There's another smile one tear
There may be darkness around you
There's always light at the end
Of the tunnel just hold on
Even if you're at the end of your tail

No, you're not in a jail
Stand up fight for freedom!
The light awaits you
At the end of the tunnel

Just live on hold on

There may be darkness around you

There's always light at the end

Of the tunnel just hold on

Even if you're at the end of your tail

They will tell us things

We won't understand

We can write our own destiny

Every corner I turn life's beating at me

You say nothing when they push you down

There may be darkness around you

There's always light at the end

Of the tunnel just hold on

Even if you're at the end of your tail

Difference
Laura Phelps, age 14

A wind of change came upon me
When I started the journey white
In the second year she came upon me
In eight things I grew
Honesty, Loyalty, Discipline, Respect
Dedication, Kindness and Responsibility

Each year I grew and come to understand
If I didn't join I'd have taken a plight
I found the strength to help others understand
White, Gold, Purple
Orange, Blue, Green, and Red

In the second year
I was selected to be in a great sight
In the third year
I joined city wide
I met new people
I saw new places

To this point
I try to do the right

To this point

I have two belts left

Red-black and black

Kindness and Responsibility

We plan to make a change

We have to fight

For hunger to change

The fight for food

Hunger to be gone

Be gone hunger

Our family

We stay tight

Stand strong family

Having each other's backs

Kick Start Kids

Kick Start Kids

Who do you want to be?

The best!

Who do you want to be?

The best!

Say it with your chest!

Kick Start Kids!

Falling Back
Laura Phelps, age 14

Who's gonna catch me when I fall

If I'm too busy not falling for everyone else

I can't think why I won't fly

I'm near the ledge someone catch me

Rocks are crumbling beneath my feet

Only seconds left 'til they

Crash beneath my feet

I'm falling now my wings clipped

No one's catching me now!

My wings are gone

The hands continue to let me fall

I'll show no pain to the ones

Who let me fall, I'll be fine

Rocks are crumbling beneath my feet

Only seconds left 'til they

Crash beneath my feet

I'm falling now my wings clipped

No one's catching me now!

A lesson we all must learn

People will let us fall

This world would never last

If we fell and never got up

Rocks are crumbling beneath my feet

Only seconds left 'til they

Crash beneath my feet

I'm falling now my wings clipped

No one's catching me now!

Even when you fall

Get back up and fly high

Don't let the hands drag you down

There's a strength for a new day

Rocks are crumbling beneath my feet

Only seconds left 'til they

Crash beneath my feet

I'm falling now my wings clipped

No one's catching me now!

Florida Beaches
Laura Phelps, age 14

The blue silver water

Just under the yonder

Under the cotton blue sky

Why would you want to say bye

Like earths heaven

Beauty illuminates from the waves

What lays beneath is a mystery

Sugar white sand

Conch shells where you hear

The song of the waves

You'd be smart to hold it dear

The blue silver water

Just under the yonder

Under the cotton blue sky

Lone Tree
Laura Phelps, age 14

(In dedication off my grandfather who passed 06/28/14)

The strong lone tree

So stubborn as can be

Life was raging for the end

But he would never leave his land

He gave all that he can

Memories both fond and grand

Loved until the end

On the outside he was hollow

On the inside he would mellow

He left with a mystery at hand

It was time for him to leave his land

But he left with a footprint in the sand

Make it a Better Place

Laura Phelps, age 14

I see everyday

The crying and hiding

The lost and alone

Sometimes they don't realize

That they're never alone

Then reach to this torturous binding

The addiction of misery

The continuation of bullying

You hear laughs and remarks

One I can't stand

"Go kill yourself." Never alone even if you're in the dark

Then begins the dark tunnel of harming

I try to help

But even my problems

Hold me down

We can all sink and swim

Everyone has issues, so hold your ground

They stay around like evil goblins

Right now is the tunnel

Going from dark to light
No matter what, you're strong
So take this stand
And win this plight

If you have a pulse
You were meant to be
If your heart beats
You have a purpose
Don't take defeat
So don't you see?

You are who you are
So don't feel weak
Smile and defeat the day
You're mightier than you think
Live your life day by day
Seek your life to the fullest

No matter who you are
I hope you reach out
And don't push people down
We are all created equal
Not to be walked on, we're not the ground
And without a doubt

I wish to make it better

Extend your hand

Everyday someone breaks

And you can't be replaced

This is nothing fake

So let's rock this in a band

The Boy Arose
Laura Phelps, age 14

Lila steps out of her desolated home and strolls to the one and only soothing place she can sketch. Her black combat boots clatter on the stone pathway as she saunters to the local Avalon cemetery. Gripping the iron bars that keep her out, she bends down to the key hole and picks her way in soon enough. They part and her safe haven is open. Usually people think cemeteries are eerie but head stones speak to her like ghostly, embracing whispers. She sits upon an aged bench that is iron green and equips her sketchpad, map pencils, and eraser so she can erase anything she wants in her own little world. The frosty, dead season's wind blows her warm white poncho. Her short, chestnut hair slaps her across the face as her shiny blue silver eyes are glued to the paper where she created her image of the flawless comrade. A male with shoulder length choppy, jet-black hair, mysterious dark brown eyes that give off a feeling of secrecy. Attired in an onyx raglan and ebony denim jeans. As he sits back, he smiles in passion with his pale pink lips that would speak uplifting words to her. Tan skin that showed his warmth and open ears to hear her cries.

Lila's long lean fingers wrap around a smooth glassy amulet passed down to her from her grand-mama and generations a fore. Her old crazy, but caring, Grammy would tell her stories about her ancestors and how she was a descendant of the Salem witches. *Grand-mama was crazy thinking this ancient thing had magical virtue*, she thought to herself.

With little hope, she whispers, "I wish that he'd come to life and be my dark prince that rescues me."

The small hand ticks to midnight on her last word and the grandfather clock cries out. Hours pass like seconds. With no motivation, she trudges to the exit as it squeaks a farewell and with that, she's off, not realizing witching hour is at hand and anything is possible.

The following day, around the same time, Lila rushes back to the graveyard where she left her beloved sketch book. Her steamy breath puffs like a train's smoke in the winter air and her talisman smacks against her chest like a ticking clock. Finally winding up at the iron gates, her breath rattles like a snake's rattler, her heart pounds like a prisoner wanting out. As she slowly gazes away, her breath is taken up once more and the prisoner escapes.

Where the note pad should have been laying, sits a boy.

The Man Behind the Mask
Laura Phelps, age 14

Click, Click, Click. I bumped around in the carriage as we rode into the clear bright night and approached a neighboring castle. Tonight was my first ball, a masquerade ball to be precise. My blue, blazing eyes pierced the celestial sphere where tiny lights danced and twinkled like the shine in someone's eyes when they're in love. My crimson blonde hair briskly snapped in the wind; I was dressed in an uncomfortable red and black raiment lined in white.

"Jessabell Jenkins! Pay attention girl!" An obnoxious voice complained in my ear.

Bluntly looking back to see my elder sister appear to be irritated.

"Huh?" I say, clueless.

"Jessabell, tonight is your first ball and you will meet your fiancé, Prince Cross. You're sixteen and have become of age *wonk... wonk... wonk... blah...* marry him. Mind your manners. It's for the kingdom, not for love, got it!?"

Staring up, lost in thought, my own questions started popping up: *What if he hates me? What kinda man will he be like? Will he rather have a mistress than be with me?*

"Oomph!" I'm shoved forward by an invisible force and before I can regain my balance. My own flesh and blood impels me out of the royal door. Before I can become gravity's victim, strong gentle arms wrap around my waist and grab hold of me.

"My... my a lady without balance a lil' clumsy aren't we ?" a warm bass voice whispers in my ear, sending tingles down my back.

I draw myself away and he grins warmly. He is a handsome, gentle man with milky brown eyes hidden behind a white mask trimmed in gold. His dark brown, trimmed hair appeared to be luscious and healthy. He towered over me like the Great Wall of China over a tree

"I'm Jessabell, Princess of Hart-land," I say, curtsying.

He chuckles and lifts up my chin. " I know who you are Princess."

This remark puzzles me. How could a stranger so mysterious know *me?*

He strode off into a sea of people. It took me moments to take in what had taken place. I sprinted after him.

"Wait! Who are you? How do you know me!?" I screech, not wanting a stranger to have my identity.

After being lost in the crowd, a few other royals impede me for a dance. My head was about to burst in wonder. The kind, queer stranger had just vanished into thin air like he ceased to exist . Between dances, I catch a glimpse of the familiar face going after him. I reach a barren area. *God he's inside my head!* I think, clearly agitated, then the man's purring voice. "I've been watching you, you seemed to be troubled miss," hearing the grin on his face.

I spin around to smack him, but it's as if no one has been near me, as if he's a figment of my imagination.

I stand there stone faced, wondering *Who was that? Was he just an illusion or was he Prince Cross?*

Tick Tock
Laura Phelps, age 14

Tick tock and I wait for now

The grinding gears of the clockwork angel

beating against my ears its wings

Bronze gears no one to hurt me now

I'm with my clockwork angel

My clockwork angel

A saving grace hear my scream

Let your beauty gleam

Bronze wings a hollow boom

Gears that grind let them sigh

Each golden cog that moves great wheel rules

Tick tock and I wait for no one

This battle has just begun

Sway into the morning with a hollow call

The salt and tears will slow my gears

Whispers mysteries in my ears

My clockwork angel

A saving grace hear my scream

Let your beauty gleam

Bronze wings a hollow boom

Gears that grind let them sigh

Each golden cog that moves great wheel rules

Battle down sing the sound
Of the clock work angel
Golden bronze sing along
You're not alone, never alone
My clockwork angel
A saving grace hear my scream
Let your beauty gleam
Bronze wings a hollow boom
Gears that grind let them sigh
Each golden cog that moves great wheel rules
Bring it on I have a clock work angel

You and Only You
Isabel Pitts, age 12

You are wondrous

You are grand

The one and only you

Which no one can compare

You and only you

Can reach for the stars

No one can bring you down

Your power and might is true

You and only you

Gruvia and Nalu – Chapter 1
Natalie Prak, age 12

It was a normal day at the guild. Noisy and tables being smashed from Grey or Natsu flown and hitting the tables. Juvia walked into the guild and was met with a flying Grey coming her way.

"Sorry Juvia, it was flame brain's fault," Grey apologized.

"It's ok Gray-sama, really, it's fine Gray-sama," Juvia reassured him.

She walked to her normal spot next to her friends, Lucy, Levy, Gajeel, and Erza. Then later, Grey and Natsu came to the table. Natsu sat next to Lucy and Grey sat down next to Juvia. Juvia clung onto his arm like always. He tried to get her off him but she wouldn't budge. He stopped and just left her on his arm. All of a sudden, a shoe hit Juvia in the head and knocked her out.

"Juvia!" Everyone yelled while running to her side!

"Gray, take Juvia home. Or else," Erza threatened him with her sword pointing to his neck.

Gray gulped and hesitated, but ended up taking her. He stood up and was off to fairy hills where Juvia stayed. Lisanna was there so he couldn't get in after she told him no boys were allowed.

Good thing that his house wasn't too far from where she lived. He had gotten to the front door when he heard Juvia say his name. She was dreaming about him.

He took out his house keys and opened the door. He went to his room, set Juvia down on his bed, and went to the kitchen to prepare a bowl with cool water and a rag. He took the rag, dipped it in the water, and placed it on Juvia's forehead. About 15 minutes later, she woke up sweating and crying Gray's name. Gray heard her scream and ran to her side. He came in knocking down the door, looking at Juvia with a worried expression.

"What's wrong Juvia? Are you ok?" he asked as he walked to the side of the bed next to her.

"N-nothing, where is Juvia?" She stuttered while asking Grey.

"You're in my house. A shoe that came out of nowhere hit you and you were knocked out so I brought you to my house and took care of you till you woke up. Not a big deal. So you don't have to worry," Gray explained to her.

Juvia blushed at the thought of her beloved taking care of her just like an old couple that love and take care of each other. "Thank you Grey-sama. Juvia really appreciates it." She gave him a heartwarming smile and he smiled back.

Grey told her that it was no problem again. She was going to leave but Grey stopped her and told her that she could spend the night since the sun was already setting. Grey gave her his clothes and she took a quick shower. Once she was done, Grey took a quick shower and Juvia was making a surprise dinner. About 30 minutes later, she was done cooking and Grey was out of the shower. He finished putting on his clothes and walked out of the bathroom.

He sniffed the air, put his dirty clothes in the hamper, and went downstairs to the kitchen where Juvia was. His mouth dropped making an 'o' shape. He looked everywhere. The food looked and smelled great.

"Grey-sama, might want to close your mouth before you catch a fly in there," she giggled.

He closed his mouth and stared at the food in amazement. It looked and smelled delightful. He helped prepare the stuff.

After they were done, they put their dirty dishes in the sink. Juvia washed everything and walked up to the room when she was finished cleaning. She walked into the room and saw Grey sound asleep. She didn't want to wake him up so she quietly walked over to bed where Grey was.

Grey sat up looking at the blue-headed girl that had stopped in her tracks, looking at him as if she was the one that had woke him up.

"If you're asking, then no, you did not wake me up I was just closing my eyes," he said, reassuring her.

"Ok." She said shyly and just kept walking towards the bed. She went under the covers next to Grey and shut her eyes.

Juvia was having a problem sleeping. She was uncomfortable and kept twisting and turning in the bed trying to sleep. Grey noticed what was happening and what she was trying to do.

"Are you ok?" he asked, turning her direction.

"Juvia just can't sleep, that's all," she told him.

He reached under her and pulled her into a tight embrace. Juvia was shocked at what just happened and all she could do was blush.

"Is that better now?" he questioned her. She nodded yes and closed her eyes.

"Ok, good night Juvia," he said to her, closing his eyes.

"Good night Grey-sama," she said to him.

Grey drifted off into dreamland where things happen the way they do, not too long after Juvia fell into a deep slumber in her beloved, Grey-sama's arms. Together they fell asleep knowing that they were safe in each other's embrace.

The Cyborg
Jesus Pulido, age 11

One day, there was a man named Bob. He was a scientist who had not accomplished very much in life. Everyday he said to himself, "What will I do?" One day, Bob saw a commercial on television that gave him a wonderful idea. His idea was to run for president. He was so excited! The election was in only one week. Bob needed to make a speech. He spent all his time and effort on the speech. He was telling all his family, friends, and neighbors to vote for him. Now there was only one day left until the election. Bob was so nervous that he started sweating all over his clothes. Finally, the day had come.

As he was giving his speech, people started yelling, "boo."

Bob was filled with so much anger that he ran off stage saying, "I'll get all of you back."

Bob spent most of his time thinking what he could do to get revenge. He thought how he could kill all the people who did not vote for him.

Bob heard who the new president was on the news. It was President Jorge. Bob wanted to kill Jorge for taking his place as president. The first time he tried to kill President Jorge, he went straight to jail, but escaped two months later. After he escaped, he finally chose what he was going to do to get back at all the people who didn't vote for him. He was going to make himself half robot. It took-months to finally finish the project. As soon as Bob was finished, he went killing innocent people only because they didn't vote for him. He said he would stop if people would make him the president. The government said they couldn't do that. Bob started to create his own army of people. His army started to kill all the people that didn't vote for him.

People were filled with fear that Bob would kill them. They started staying inside their homes and no one came out. After everything that had happened, they decided to make Bob the new president. Bob stopped killing people and the world was a better place, but after two months, the country was falling apart with Bob as the president. He thought that things were better with him as the president. Later, he realized things were actually getting worse so he said that he didn't want to be president anymore.

One day, he said, "I quit."

When he quit, they made Jorge the president again. When Jorge was done being president, Bob decided to try being president again, but he lost to Jorge again. Bob got very angry and started to rob banks. Police tried to catch him, but Bob was too good of a criminal.

Finally, one day police caught him shopping at the store. When he tried to escape jail this time police caught him and locked him up in a special room. Every day he tried to escape, but he just couldn't. The police started to say that the world would be so much better without Bob. The police decided to eliminate Bob once and for all. Bob insisted they let him live, but they didn't listen. The day had come. There would be no more disasters. The police injected Bob with poison, then he died.

Recovery
Sabrina Ramirez, age 14

The stars shined brightly in the dark night sky as I sat on the terrace thinking about her. Thoughts, memories, and flashbacks raced in my head. I lazily picked myself up, dragging my feet across the cement floor. As I shut the glass door, my mother startled me. She looked drained of energy and upset. Of course, it's because of me.

"Luke," she said almost sounding like a whisper.

I tilted my head. I stopped talking after *she* died.

"This is going to be extremely hard for me but I think you should go live with your father for a while."

My father? He hasn't been with me for nine *years! Why would she decide this?* I ran my fingers through my blonde hair and stared at my mother with wide eyes.

Her used-to-be bright blue eyes were dull and full of sorrow. I just nodded slightly to make her happy. She gave me her best smile and left my room. I closed the door and slid my body down the wall. So many frustrating things in my mind. I took out my journal where I wrote songs or poems. I searched for a clear page and wrote something that came to mind.

"Torn, in two, and I know I shouldn't tell you, but I just can't stop thinking of you. Wherever you are."

My tears fell onto the paper, smearing the black ink. Slamming the journal closed, I threw it across my dark, depressing room. Tears ran down my face as I thought, *Why? Why did she have to go? Why couldn't it be me instead of her?* Why, why, why is all that came across my mind.

I awoke to soft, quiet knocks on my door. I slowly lifted myself off my bed and opened the door revealing my two idiotic friends.

"Rise and shine, Lukey," they said in unison.

I rubbed the slumber out of my eyes and slightly waved.

"Your mom called us to help you pack," Calum spoke.

I tapped on Michael's shoulder and pointed to my phone, signaling if he could hand me my phone. He nodded and placed my phone in the palm of my hand.

We rummaged through all my junk, trying to stuff everything we could in my two suitcases. I laid in my bed not even sure where my father lived. I clicked on my voice app on my phone and typed.

"Can you guys get my mom up?" the robotic voice said.

They nodded and left my room. Out of the corner of my eye, I saw a picture on the floor. I walked over, picked it up, and instantly regretted it. It was of her. Tears welled up in my eyes as I remembered the day Calum took the picture.

My anxiety grew higher and higher. As I reached for my medication, both Calum, Michael, and my mother walked in my room. They knew I could get worse. I popped two pills in my mouth and gulped down a glass of water. Both my friends and mother calmed down.

With the question of where my father was located, I wrote on a crumbled piece of paper. "Mom, where does my father live?" I handed her the piece of paper.

She sighed and looked at me. "He lives in New York, hun," she replied.

I was going to New York!

"By the way, your flight leaves tomorrow."

And just like that, I was on a one way plane ride to New York. I placed my luggage in the carry-on and took my seat next to this adorable little girl.

She smiled at me and said, "Hi, I'm Delilah!"

I waved at her and slightly smiled.

"What's your name?" Delilah asked.

I typed on my phone for a few seconds. "My name is Luke and Delilah is a beautiful name," said my voice app.

She looked confused at first but then smiled. A girl about my age sat next to the little girl.

"I'm back, Delilah," said the girl.

Delilah nodded and closed her eyes. The girl smiled at me. She looked exactly like my last love. "Hey, I'm Ariella."

I froze. Never in my life did I want to hear that name again. A flashback of Arielle and I came to mind. I shook my head coming back from my flashback of her. As I slightly waved to Ariella, I turned my head looking towards my feet. It had been countless hours of avoiding Ariella until we finally landed in New York. I quickly hopped out of my seat and gathered my luggage. Loads of people were crowding the airport. As I pushed through the crowds, I spotted my father. My eyes instantly rolled in annoyance as I walked up to him. He smiled and embraced me in a hug. I awkwardly patted his back.

"Um, let's get going. I want you to meet my neighbor's daughters that also came from Australia today."

We both made our way through the airport and walked up to a BMW. I plopped myself in the passenger's seat and fiddled with my lip ring.

"Does your mother let you wear that thing?" he asks.

I just shrugged and made this annoyed face as we drove through New York. We reached this apartment complex and parked in a two-story garage. My father took my two suitcases out and made his way inside the complex.

My father's apartment number is 118. We entered the semi-expensive apartment.

"Want anything to eat, bud?' he asks.

Bud? Are you kidding me? I raised my eyebrows and shook my head "no" since I stopped eating much after her death.

"Okay then... Your room is the room to the right."

I dragged my suitcases with me inside the dark blue room. As I sat on the edge of the bed, my dad walked in the room. *Geez, let me breathe.*

"C'mon we're um.. going next door ," he said.

Woo-hoo, socializing my favorite thing to do! Note the sarcasm. I rolled my eyes and pushed past him, hitting his shoulder a bit.

We made our way to the next-door neighbor's. My father knocked on the door and waited a few seconds for the door to open. Once the door opened, I looked up to see Ariella at the door.

"Hi Mr. Hemmings! So good to see you again," she said.

We made eye contact as my father greeted her. "Hey, aren't you that boy from the plane?"

I looked up and of course it's Ariella. I nodded slightly.

"Cool, welcome to New York!"

She reminds me so much of Arielle. It's like they're freaking sisters! I'm not going to recover if she reminds me so much of her. It's all my fault she's gone. My dad interrupted my thoughts asking if I was okay. I nodded, *well here goes the socializing.*

It's now been about a month of me living here with basically the same routine I had in Australia. Countless therapy appointments, writing in my journal, and staying in the tiny room my dad has. I've been trying to ignore everybody. The only time I come out of my room is to look outside or to get something I need.

Quiet knocks were at my door. I didn't bother using my voice app or opening the door since whoever would walk in anyway. In walked Ariella with her hands stuffed inside her hoodie pocket.

"Hey," she said.

I waved as I looked down at my cat print socks.

"Nice socks, Blondie."

I smiled faintly.

"Um, your dad wanted me to make sure you took your pills already."

My heart rate accelerated as I looked at the three pill containers sitting on the nightstand.

"You haven't been taking this one," she said, lifting a container.

I gulped.

"What does this one help for?"

I looked into her hazel green eyes that were similar to Arielle's. I took my phone out and typed. "It's to be happy," the lame robotic voice said.

"Why don't you want to be happy?" she asked.

I typed once again. "I don't deserve to be happy."

She looked away and wiped the tears brimming in her eyes.

"My life is a silent hurricane. Nobody can see how much her passing hurt me," I typed for Ariella to hear.

"How did she die?"

My heart ached as I remembered the day she died. "It's my fault she's dead. It's all my fault she got into that stupid car crash! She was texting me while driving that night. I remember the last time we held a conversation perfectly. The last time I ever heard her voice was in the voicemail she sent before coming over," my voice app spoke. Tears slid down my face as I looked up to see Ariella's face.

She wiped away her constant spilling tears. "Let me help you. Let me show you that you'll recover, but of course remember the passing of your sweetheart," she said.

I nodded, agreeing to recover, not only for my friends and family, but for Arielle too.

Four months. That's how long I've been in New York now. Remember how I was willing to let Ariella help me recover? Yeah, well the best part is that she managed to help me recover. I, Luke Hemmings, recovered, beating all of my demons.

I'm now flying back to Australia to visit her. Yes, Arielle, the love of my life that tragically passed. As soon as I landed, I drove straight to the cemetery. I walked a few acres before I reached her tombstone.

I smiled as I ran my fingers across her name. "Hey, beautiful. You have no idea how much I missed you."

As I opened my journal, I sat down next to her and tilted the page "Amnesia."

"If today I woke up with you right beside me. Like all of this was just some twisted dream. I'd hold you closer than I've ever did before. And you'd never slip away and you'd never hear me say." I smiled as I closed my journal. "You would be so proud of what I overcame. I love you. You'll always have a special place in my heart," I spoke aloud hoping she would hear. And with that, I kissed her tombstone and sang our song we wrote together.

"You're never gonna be alone, from this moment on. If you ever feel like letting go, I won't let you fall."

Albert Finsley
Sandy Ramirez, age 12

Albert Finsley was the first person to ever be changed from a human to a robot. His purpose was to help the world of science, technology, and learning at first, but one day, there was a small change of plans.

Once Albert was changed, people no longer treated him like a human being—even though technically he wasn't—but the saddest part was, he didn't even notice. And as time passed by, more people started treating him like an object.

A party was held at the Laboratory of Technology and Discovery and—no surprise here—Albert wasn't invited. Of course though, like all things, it was found out. And once it was, he was furious! Sort of, at first he was pretty angry, but then, he was a little confused. It had been a long time since Albert had gotten mad and the emotion seemed very foreign to him.

After a while, Albert realized what was going on. To others, he was no longer a person, just a piece of metal used for work. But he knew he was more than that. He was once human, and even though now most of his body was metal and nails, he could still feel. His emotions were very real and Albert decided to show them that.

Albert started rebelling. He refused to do what they told him to do. He knew he might be shut down, since the others thought he was malfunctioning, but they were too scared to find out. So they left him alone since he wasn't really hurting anyone.

But one day, another human went through with the transformation. Albert was beyond furious, he was enraged! He absolutely loathed the other scientists for what they were doing. But before he could give them a piece of his mind, Albert came up with a plan. Rebelling obviously wouldn't make the scientists see the wrong they were doing, so he decided he would do what he was made for. He decided to help the world of science, technology, and learning, just not in the way it was expected. These "robots" that were being used without any appreciation or acknowledgement, they were human too.

Heart Field
Sandy Ramirez, age 12

Not So Sunshine Hotel
Nadiya Richardson, age 11

It was a sunny spring morning and Gloria went outside to get the mail. Eddie came downstairs to kiss her on the cheek since they were just engaged. She found a brochure in the mail and the brochure said, "Come to Sunshine Hotel and you will just die experiencing just how awesome it is here." Gloria went to Eddie and gave him the brochure and they decided that they would go there to relax and have a fun time.

That won't last very long....

The hotel was located in Sunshine Falls. As they arrived, they noticed that the hotel looked nothing like it did in the brochure. On the brochure it looked bright and happy, but when they arrived, it looked like the total opposite of the brochure. The hotel looked raggedy and torn up. Eddie wanted to go back home, but somehow Gloria convinced him to stay.

Gloria said, "It took three and a half hours to get here and we are not going back home. And anyways, we have coupons from the brochure."

So they went to check in and no one was there. After waiting for fifteen unbearable minutes, they turned their heads around and out of nowhere, a person appeared at the front desk. It was a very petite, elderly woman who had little round glasses on the tip of her nose. She was extremely pale. Eddie asked the lady for the biggest room.

While on the way there, they saw a colossal red stain in front of their room door. "There was a murder here in 1997 in the front of this room and two little boys died. Sometimes you can see their spirits playing with a ball in this hallway around two or three in the morning, but they don't hurt anybody," the old woman said.

So they went into the room and began to unpack. While they were unpacking, they heard a bang in the back of the hotel and Eddie went outside to investigate. When he got outside, in the back of the hotel he saw a hand sticking out of the ground. He ran for his life and as he was running, he heard someone scream. He ran back into his hotel room and Gloria was screaming. She couldn't get the words out of her mouth; she was mumbling. She pointed to the bed so Eddie picked up the covers and there was another colossal red stain, and also a knife. The knife was so sharp, if you even tapped it on your arm you would start bleeding. He rushed downstairs and told the elderly lady about the hand, blood, and the knife in the bed. She told him to calm down and all of a sudden the lights went out. When the lights came back on, the lady was gone. Eddie ran upstairs to get Gloria. He told her to pack her things so they could leave; Gloria tried to pack up everything as fast as she could. When everything was packed up, they ran downstairs and as soon as they stepped outside the hotel, the hotel started shaking uncontrollably. They climbed into the car and the engine wouldn't work. Then the elderly woman ran out of the hotel with a stab wound in her arm.

She screamed, "This hotel was built on a graveyard!"

Gloria screamed like she just saw a mountain lion about to pounce on her. Eddie went to the shed in the back of the hotel. As he ran, a hand came out of the ground and grabbed his ankle. He screamed for Gloria. Gloria tried to pull him, but the hand that was clutching onto his ankle was too strong. Every time the hand pulled, he went deeper and deeper into the ground. Gloria got out her cell phone to try to call someone, but unfortunately she couldn't pick up a signal. They said their last goodbyes. She kissed him on the forehead and after that, he was already underground. He was gone. She cried hysterically until the elderly woman came to comfort her.

"My name is Patty," the elderly woman said.

Patty realized that there was a rotary phone in the hotel. Gloria was brave enough to go and get it. When she walked inside, everything was broken because of the hotel shaking. She found the rotary phone and called the police. The police showed up after five minutes. She told the police about what happened and they were stunned. The police had investigators come and check it out. They checked everywhere. They hired workers to break down the hotel. When they were done, there was a massive graveyard. There were hundreds of people buried there.

The investigators said that some nuclear waste spilled all over the graveyard which caused the hotel to shake and it made that person come alive that attacked Eddie.

Their families were shocked when they heard the news about Eddie's horrible tragedy. Gloria went home and gathered all of the pictures she had of Eddie for the memorial service. When she had the service for him, everybody was devastated. Gloria and Patty's relationship grew closer after the funeral. They almost saw each other every weekend. Gloria said she will never forget that day as long as she lives.

The Kingdom of Beast and King
Ilda Rivera, age 12

The Psychic Fortune Cookie
Haley Rodriguez, age 12

"Would you like a fortune cookie?" the waiter asked.

"Yes, please," Soyla replied.

"Here you go, ma'am," the waiter said.

"Thank you." Soyla broke the fortune cookie in half with curiosity. CRACK. Soyla unrolled the piece of paper.

It read, "Your life is in great danger!"

Soyla was surprised by what it said but she didn't listen. The girl crumpled up the piece of paper, thinking nothing of it, then threw it on the ground as she hopped in a cab.

The very next day, Soyla got out of bed to get ready for work right before the doorbell rang. Soyla went to open the door to see nobody there. She was confused, she looked left, then right, then peered down to see a fortune cookie sitting on her porch. She picked up the fortune cookie and broke it in half.

It read, "Do not go to work today."

Though she was tempted to stay, Soyla ignored the cookie. She continued to get ready only to change her mind and stay home. Soyla turned on the news. There had been a shooting at her job and it was on the same floor her office was. Soyla was mortified about what had happened at her job. If she had gone to work, her life might have ended. Soyla realized the fortune cookies were true. She woke up the next morning to a knock on the door. It was the mailman with a package.

"One package for Ms. Soyla."

She took the package out of his hand even though she was not expecting a package. Soyla opened the box. It was a fortune cookie.

She broke the cookie in half to see a paper that said, "Don't take a shower."

Because of what happened the last time, Soyla did not take a shower.

"Thank God, I didn't take a shower!" Soyla yelled.

She later found out that people who had used the water were brutally burned. There had been acid in the water because of a chemical spill. Soyla was relieved that she listened to the cookie. Soyla heard all this talk about a big storm so she prepared for it. It was all over the news. Soyla was so busy preparing that she didn't realize the fortune cookies stopped showing up at her house. She thought that maybe the fortune cookies would stop, but she was wrong.

On the day of the big storm, Soyla heard a knock on her door. She saw another fortune cookie that said, "Stay home." Soyla already knew to stay home. She knew that if she stepped foot outside, her life would be in peril. Soyla planned to stay in her bathroom the whole storm. Soyla was all packed and prepared. She could hear the thunder. She also heard a dog barking outside. She peered out the window to see a small dog stuck in her rose bush. Though the fortune cookie said to stay inside, she was fighting the urge to help the dog. Soyla couldn't bear to know that the dog's life could end because she didn't help it. She had a big decision to make. Would she save the dog or listen to the fortune cookie that had been right all along? Soyla could see the storm, but she decided to follow her heart and save the dog.

Soyla ran outside, quickly released the dog, and ran inside with him cradled in her arms. She turned to see the storm fading away. The next thing she knew, she heard a knock on the door. She opened the door to a fortune cookie.

It read: "Good job. All you needed was a wise decision you made yourself. You followed your heart."

Soyla was relieved and was surprised to hear those words. Never again will she order fortune cookies, ever.

Robotic Emotions
Katherine Rodriguez, age 12

Mr. Pedro wanted to create something and *be* someone. He researched what he needed, bought the materials, and decided that he was ready. On the first day, he started building the two legs. The following day, he created the arms. Day after day, coffee after coffee, Dr. Pedro was finishing his new and unique creation. The project was done in just two stressful months…but there was a problem… he didn't want anyone to know about his new robotic creation. His creation could never see the forsaken world of the outside…

He was unaware that this wasn't completely true. Roy, as named by its creator, accidentally stumbled upon a forest after escaping its "room" through the window. It seemed boring and even dangerous, but something caught the inexperienced machine's eye—or bionic lenses in this case.

"Salut." Though programmed with more than 150 different languages, Roy had trouble with which language was the one mainly used in this mysterious land. "Konichiwa, kaixo, zdravstuyte, xin chao? Hallo…Hello?" It didn't matter what language he tried using, the strangers didn't understand. "Aydia. Estiaios perimnas." The strangers spoke an unknown dialect to Roy. He wasn't programmed for this language.

Roy could only communicate as best it could. "I-I don't understand what you are saying. Are you lost? Are you able to speak a different language? Noz estiaios perimnas. Noi saios e dont estiaios. Nous podrinsa aydiaa?"

The strangers were still speaking their mysterious language.

Roy wasn't sure what to do. "I really can't understand what you are saying, but…" Roy remembered his owner and believed that it was the best choice. "I can take you to my owner if you guys want—well you can't actually understand me. Just follow me."

With a gesture, Roy took the two strangers back to the room it escaped from. Roy led the strangers to the back of the kitchen where a simple fridge stood. Roy went behind it and pulled a hidden lever. A huge opening appeared suddenly on the wall next to the fridge. Inside, was a very large white room with several objects and beakers with colorful substances in them. Roy went in and signaled the strangers to stay outside. Deep into the room stood a man in a white lab coat who turned as he was approached by the robot.

"Hey, what are you doing here?" Mr. Pedro was perplexed. Why was his creation was in his laboratory?

Roy replied, "Well…I found…"

"Yes?" He rushed the robot, for he was very busy.

"Well, I found two strangers."

"And?" Roy continued.

"They don't look like you…"

The man simply scoffed. "Well, of course not! I don't have any siblings!"

"N-no." Roy tried its best to explain the situation. "They don't look like you, or anyone else you told me were people."

"I don't understand."

Roy took the man to the outside of the lab, and could only look at the man with an astonished face. Roy could barely catch what the man said under his breath.

"Aliens…"

Two years passed since the discovery of what seemed to be true extraterrestrials. Unfortunately, media soon caught on…

A knock on the door disrupted the early breakfast of the four individuals in the household. Mr. Pedro got up from his chair and walked to the door, only to be surprised by an unexpected man.

"Greetings!" The unexpected guest came in, wearing a blue coat, top hat, white pants, a redwood-carved cane, and about 280 pounds of pure fat. He also had a goat for some reason…The average stereotype of a mayor, I guess?

"T'is I, Mayor Greenbacks of...What tow-Oh, yeah! Townsville!" The man replied with a chuckle. "You mean Downsville"

"Y-Yes! Exactly! Mayor of...Downsville! Mm..."

"And...What brings you here mayor?"

"Well simple, actually, I came for your need."

"My need?" Mr. Pedro wasn't sure what the mayor meant by "need."

"Yes! Indeed I do! You see, my last secretary was a very nasty person—to the people I mean—in behavior. I don't mean nasty as in her never showering or—" Noticing he was getting off task, he got back on topic. "Anyways, she was the tenth secretary I had to fire, and it occurred to me...that um...that I can never find the perfect secretary and decided that—"

The delightful mayor was halted by Mr. Pedro. "Mayor...I don't roll that way..."

Mayor Greenbacks was a bit confused, but simply replied with a hardy laugh. "OH! No, no! I don't mean to make you a secretary! No— Just no...well...I won't mind you helping me on some paperwork—"

"I'm sorry, sir"

"Oh, no that's fine. All fine. I actually meant as in a *robotic* secretary. You being an engineer and all..."

"You mean to tell me if I could make a fake secretary for you?"

"Yes! Yes! Ha-ha! I would kindly appreciate it! You think you could?"

"Yes. It'll keep me busy."

"Perfect! Now how much do you charge?" The mayor was taking out his checkbook.

"No, no mayor. There is no need."

"But I insist." The mayor was unable to convince the man of payment and finally gave up. Before leaving, the mayor looked back at the man, and said, "You're a good man, Mr. Pedro. Maybe enough to be the next mayor... please don't take my job."

Pedro simply replied, "Don't worry mayor."

Mayor Greenbacks was so excited with the new secretary, that he recommended it to the governor, but the mayor didn't realize what he had done.

The governor sent seven guys to look for Mr. Pedro and talk to him about the recommendation. They took him to the governor and he decided what he was going to do to him.

"I really don't have time, but would you work with me? I will pay you as much as you want."

"I really don't know. I will think about it. I will have an answer tomorrow."

After two days, the governor went to look for him. Impatiently waiting at the front door, knocking and knocking over and over again, Mr. Pedro finally opened the door.

"Come in," Pedro insisted.

When the governor went inside, he found the aliens! He sneaked out the house with the aliens but he didn't realize that Roy was following him. But the governor soon found out and kept Roy as well. The governor had made a decision to keep the aliens and Roy. But on that day, Roy found that before leaving the house, the governor had killed Pedro. So Roy changed. For some reason, he felt like he needed revenge.

Roy was put on sale and soon he wasn't at the sale, but outside the governor's office with the aliens.

My True Friends
Maryfer Rodriguez, age 12

Friends come and go, but not always. Some of my friends I met were from elementary school and some of my friends I met in middle school. My best friend and I met before we both went to elementary school and her name is Emily. Emily and I did almost everything together. Her mom would work and my mom would take of us or the other way around, but when school started Emily ended up going to another school so we got separated. We forgot all about each other. At the end of the third grade year, her family moved in by where I lived so my sister and her sister, since they are good friends, took us to the park nearby. We were both in an awkward position since we thought that we didn't know each other, but after a while of being in the park, we ended up becoming friends again. That summer was really fun and we had just found out that she was going to be transferred to my school and we were both so excited.

When we went to meet our fourth grade, we found out that we weren't in the same class, but fourth grade went by fast and that summer went by fast too. Fifth grade was one of the most fun years I had. My friends, including Emily, were in my class, but it was also one of the saddest years because it was going to be our last year of elementary school and we were all going to different schools. The end of the year was the hardest.

I still remember my mom getting a call from the magnet coordinator saying that I had just been accepted to Johnston and he said that he would give me some time to decide. I never thought I would come to Johnston, but I still came to audition. I decided to try something new and different. I accepted my offer to come to Johnston. When I told Emily and another friend of ours, Fany, that I was going to Johnston, Fany was really mad and that's where our friendship started to end. The end of the school year came and our friendship ended. That summer was weird because it was only Emily and I and we were both going to different schools but we also tried to have fun that summer, but the first day of school came all of the sudden.

It felt as if everything went by fast. I didn't know anyone and surely they didn't know me. I saw that everyone had their own friends and I didn't even know one person. I felt that it was going to be hard for me to make friends and I just wanted to go to my zoned school where I knew half the kids there. But little by little, I started to make friends and I started to enjoy going to school. All my teachers are nice, forgiving, and always help me when I don't understand something. I've met a lot of new people and I enjoy coming to school. Mackenzie, she always helps me in math because she is really good and she is just a fun and interesting person to hang out with. Maggie and Alina are very unique and talented friends and are very fun people to hang out with. Emari is a friend I can trust and who I can tell anything to. Jonathan, Romo, and Mario, who, even though they get on my nerves, are fun and entertaining people. Andy and Joshua, people who I can talk to in Spanish and who help me with anything I ask them to help me with. Last, but not least, Eric and Chase make me laugh with the simplest things and just make me feel happy when I'm sad or frustrated.

At the beginning of the year I felt out of place because I didn't know anyone, but now I feel like I belong somewhere. I don't regret coming to Johnston anymore because I didn't lose friends by coming here. I made even more who are just fun and caring people to be with. And the teachers are also people who care about their students like Ms. Mitchell, Ms. Stutts, Ms. Carrion, Ms. Braxton, and Mr. Cowan. Teachers who help me every way possible to pass and Ms. Kennedy, Ms.Conner, and Ms. Arlt who are my magnet and gym teachers who are, like all my teachers, people I can trust. I love being at school and having fun all the time with all my friends.

Dedicated to Ms.Mitchell and all my friends for inspiring me.

Happy Life
Sky Rodriguez, age 13

Out of Time

Jonathan Rojas, age 12

Boom! Gunshots could be heard in the distance. Robert told George, Ellie, and Rose to turn off the TV. Robert did not want them to watch the news while the war was going on, but they did not listen. George and Ellie tried to convince him to watch the news, but he had already started building something. Later, they wondered what Robert was building. It was some kind of device, and he would not tell them. The next day, Robert told them he built a time machine. They didn't believe him, so Robert showed it to them.

George couldn't wait to use the time machine and go back in time. Rose was a little scared of travelling back in time. Eventually, they all decided to travel back in time. They each wanted to do something or meet someone from the past. Robert wanted to go back in time and meet Albert Einstein. George quickly decided he should go next, he had always wanted to go back in time and visit castles and kings and knights and so they did. Ellie thought about it for a while and then thought she could go back in time to when she was in 1st grade and give her five-year-old self a pep talk about how to stop the bigger kids from bullying her. Rose did not want to use the machine at all; she knew something would likely go wrong. They were all having a good time using the machine, and then Robert got an idea about using the time machine to stop the war. They all knew the story of how the war began in the first place, so it would be easy to go back to that time and stop it.

Years ago, when he was little, President JJ had stolen another kid's lollipop. That kid ended up becoming President Ishmael, the president of the country next to their own and he had never forgotten that his lollipop had been stolen. From the first day his lollipop was stolen, he declared he would have his revenge on JJ. Therefore, they decided to go back in time and prevent this from happening. Robert, George, Ellie, and Rose jumped into the time machine and went back in time to that day. When they appeared, they saw President JJ had already taken the lollipop away from the future president Ishmael. They all ran towards them with a plan in mind. They would break the lollipop in half, and give both of them a piece. When they got back to the present, it was like no time had passed. They all rushed to the TV to see if the news was on and to see if they had stopped the war from happening. They saw that it had worked because there was no talk about any wars in their town on the news.

As they started to celebrate, they heard the TV reporter say that it had been the worst month ever. Last week, an enormous forest fire took lives. The week before, a bad train wreck had occurred and today there was a devastating plane crash with 300 people aboard. The plane crashed into another plane in the middle of their flight. Their plan to stop the war had worked, but it had made other bad things happen. Rose, Robert, and Ellie all looked worried, but not George. He told them they shouldn't worry since they had the time machine. It could fix all bad events that had occurred. They all decided they should give it a try, after all what's the worst thing that could happen?

The Crow
Braden Schepp, age 13

The Sky I See
Isis Salas, age 12

So dark and cold it is in here
Covered by darkness, nothing else
Watching the sky cry, Makes me feel bad
Why are you crying I ask?

I go to my bed to sleep

Two hours later, I wake up
Happiness and light is all I can see
Who made you happy? I ask
Never mind I say,
I'm just glad someone made you happy a

Just one drop...
Can mean alot...

Excerpt from Earth Ascending
Lauren Sternenberg, age 12

My name is Atalisk Hazel Marie Boulden. I am a princess. No, I used to be a princess. My kingdom was destroyed by the Flame. I should be dead. I was the only survivor out of our province.

I surveyed the apple groves from my cloaked and secluded perch. The apple groves were my source of food since all of the castle provisions were completely burned from the Flame. I clenched my fists, my nails biting into the soft, yet worn, flesh. My bow was gripped in my left hand, the accompanying arrows in a quiver resting upon my back. My small emergency flee pack, EFP for short, hung on my royal sash. My EFP contained a piece of the Neverending Feast Tablecloth, which was only for emergencies since it could only provide enough for approximately one meal per day, buffet style, and only for three more years until it's magic was exhausted. My EFP also had some herbs for illnesses, a map of the twelve provinces, enchanted to show them three dimensionally and give an interactive panorama of where I wished to go. It also had three teleport seeds; if you had to make an emergency escape, you would picture where you wish to go and smash the seed by stomping on it. It held an enchanted goblet, which provided endless water, and a small weapon of choice. Mine was a battle axe. Finally, there was a small book, one that told of legends of the Flame and every myth and story of our ancestors, the Forest Sylphs. It guided us under the paths of the various heroes destined to banish the Flame. The mother of all Forest Sylphs, Flora, was said to have blessed each book with fortune and luck. Oh, please.

Even so, I cherished my EFP and was grateful that I always wore this sash with it attached. I also forgot that my quiver was enchanted to always replenish my arrows. Normal arrows took about two seconds to form, fire arrows took about five seconds, water arrows took about seven seconds, wind took nine, normal earth ones took eleven seconds, and Blessed Arrows of Earth, BAEs for short, took about thirty seconds. My quiver held up to fifty arrows. I only got these enchanted items because I was the youngest princess of the now destroyed kingdom of Ethenia. They were for survival, including trading money: Ihrani. Thran for one. I had a small fortune's worth of trading and living Ihrani.

I clutched the cloak around my shoulders, glad for the comfort it still gave. It was a woodsy camouflage print with insulation of grizzly bear fur on the inside. It had a drawstring hood that covered my now useless tiara. It was pure gold with small sapphire ornamentation. It acted as an intricately woven bangle against my, also golden, hair. I gripped my bow tighter as I watched a herd of deer run through the field just past my apple orchard. My hazel eyes scanned for predators nearby, yet saw none currently eyeing the same prey as me. I positioned my gold and silver bow and drew a regular arrow from my quiver, watching a big buck who stood slightly away from the rest of the group. I aimed and heard the wind rustling the long grass as my Sylphears twitched. I pulled back the string and watched the buck raise its mighty head, aiming for a quick and painless death. Just as I was about to fire, I heard something rustling right above me, slightly behind my line of sight. I stiffened, then let the string go. The buck fell, and I felt something grab my shoulders. I whirled, my battle axe raised at the figure. They stumbled, and their black hood fell back. Vivid green eyes met mine, and I flinched at the sudden contact.

"Why did you fire?" he asked, gripping my shoulders a bit harder, causing a gasp of pain to leave my lips. His eyes softened, and his grip loosened. "Why would you do that?" he inquired, his voice also softer; wispy and musical opposed to his previous tone. I gulped, knowing that I didn't have a great answer.

"I did it so I can eat; so I can survive. I don't just shoot animals for sport," I say. He lets go of my shoulders and scoots next to me on my tree branch. We sit in silence for a minute or so, until I get up and jump from the branch to collect my kill. "I can't waste food. Not at a time like this."

"Need help?" he asks, and I begin to shake my head, but stop once I realize that there is no way I can consume this meat alone before it spoils. I then turn back to him, see his caramel brown locks covering his eyes, and I can't help but feel a twinge of guilt. It definitely doesn't help that he looks a lot like my younger brother, Adryen, who was kidnapped when I was thirteen and he was twelve. I still haven't forgiven myself for letting him out of my sight.

"Actually, I could use some help ..." I trail off, waiting for his name. He catches on and whispers,

"Rin, just Rin."

"Well okay, 'Rin just Rin', would you help me break this beast down and prepare him for dinner? I'm inviting you," I offer. Honestly, he looked as if he hadn't had a decent meal in a few weeks. His short, jaw-length hair was dirty and wild, sticking up in different areas, while his face had dirt speckled on his cheekbones. His backpack was ripped in certain areas, covered in mud, and seemingly empty. I see a smile flash across his face, and he rubs the back of his neck awkwardly.

"Well, okay. I'll accept your invitation and help you prepare the deer, but can I take half the leftovers for my pack? I ran out of food rations about five days ago and haven't found anything even close to edible. If not, I don't mind," he trailed off self-consciously, and I noticed the tips of his pointed ears were a bright red, and his cheeks a dark pink. I chuckled, grabbed his wrist, and dragged him towards the carcass. I sat down next to it and clapped my hands together, facing him cross-legged.

"So, how do you do this?"

The Night
Madeline Strug, age 11

A blank canvas floats on air as night slowly loses light.
A large silver crescent floats above me.
Bright stars fill the canvas and sing a song of joy.
A yellow light rises and the stars and moon disappear.
The canvas is blank Ready to be created once again.

War of the Realms
Han Truong, age 11

I wore a dark hood that concealed my face as I walked through the village. All the villagers stared at me as if I had killed most of their people—which I may have done—and they were all silent. I hastened my steps as I neared the exit of the village.

Then, a guard stopped me and asked, "What is your name?"

"Must I tell you my name to leave?" I responded.

"There have been several murders, all committed by an assassin. It's for the protection of this village," he responded.

I quickly thought of a fake name and said, "My name is Sarah."

The guard looked at me suspiciously. Then he said, "Full name."

I tried to think of another name, then I responded, "Sarah Silas Goldman."

The guard opened the door and let me through. I sighed in relief. I smirked, surprised that he didn't find out I was the assassin. My real name is Kira; I recently found out that the Four Realms are having a conflict about some creatures crossing over each other's borders.

I need to cross the "battlefield" or the center—where they all meet—so I can get to where Aunt Zelda is. Both my mother and father passed away, but I was told I had a lost older brother. As I continued walking through the forest, I heard the growl of a wolf. I froze and tried not to make any sudden movements. My hand was on the hilt of my sword. I looked into the eyes of the wolf; they were red.

"I've never seen a wolf with red eyes before..." I muttered.

Then, the wolf pounced and everything went black.

I was in a cave, where a fire was made. As I got up, I felt an excruciating pain in my side and arm. I saw a boy that sat across from me.

"You're awake," he said.

I got up and slowly walked to the entrance of the cave to leave.

"Where are you going?" he said.

"To the Four realms." I responded.

He looked at me funny. "Not in that condition you're not." he said. "My name is Keiro," he continued.

I narrowed my eyes, "Why would you care?"

I saw his cold smile. "Were you too weak to fight the wolf?" he said.

I looked up at him and gritted my teeth. "No, It was just..," I paused not remembering what I did. "Anyways," I tried to change the subject, "The wolf s eyes were red."

He said, "Another tainted wolf..."

"That wolf was tainted?" I said, thinking about its red eyes.

"Yes, of course. Its eyes were red and usually they are stronger than regular wolves," he responded.

"How did it become tainted?" I asked.

"Poisons from the Dark Realm may have gotten in the water and other resources. As a result, most of the wild life may have been contaminated," he said.

I walked out of the cave with him. His name sounded familiar. I grasped my thoughts and continued walking.

After a few minutes of walking, I looked ahead again and saw the Earth Realm. I ran ahead and the forest seemed abandoned and silent. After a while, I thought, *is Keira my lost brother?*

"Shh...," He interrupted.

I looked at what he was looking at and saw the life in all four realms clustered together, yet the element of which they belonged to was still detectable.

The war was about to begin.

The Secret Elixir
Madeline Vanlandingham, age 12

Why do bad things always happen to me? I wonder, as I get struck by green lightning. Again.

I've memorized what happens next. First, I'll see glowing snakes, my mortal enemies. Next, I'll start hearing eerie flute music. Finally, I'll faint, but that doesn't happen this time. I just fall to the floor, unconscious.

When I wake up, I feel a strange wriggling feeling on my head. I slowly creep across the floor of my cave towards my mirror and as soon as I see what the source of the wriggling is, I almost faint again. My dark brown hair has been transformed into a mass of wriggling, green, venomous, evil-looking snakes. Fabulous! After the shock of having snakes for hair dies down, I sneak another peek in the mirror. My eyes are now green with pupils like a snake's, and my skin has a greenish tinge that no amount of concealer will be able to cover.

"Curse you, Athena," I shout to nobody at all, besides Athena, of course. I will eternally have to look like a mutant, seasick anaconda. Yay! Thanks a lot, Athena. Whoo hoo! So happy, NOT!

Oh, Gods, what will my mom say? Oh, wait, I don't have a mom. She died in a fire so I ran away. I don't talk of her much. The last thing she said to me was, "Remember my story." My mom meant the story of the magic elixir that could reverse anything.

"That's it!" I yell, again to nobody at all.

I pack up my whole cave and venture out into the stormy night with a veil on my head, looking like a widow or something. I'm too young to look like that. I'm only fifteen! The next morning I come to a nearby town. I hope nobody notices me. They'll ask questions and the like, and I'll be all sarcastic and such when answering them. It's the way I am.

"Oh, Gods," I mutter.

There's a dark dot rushing at me. It gets closer and soon I can see its figure. "About six feet high, seven feet long with a pitch black mane and tail with silver highlights. I'd say...a nightmare," I say to nobody in particular. "I thought they were all extinct." It's the most beautiful creature I have ever seen!

"Well, you're wrong," says a voice. "They aren't all extinct. They just went into hiding."

I look up, pondering the source of the voice, and I see tanned skin, poppy-red lips, high cheekbones, vivid, blue eyes, and a mop of black hair. I'm in like! Snap out of it, Medusa. Snap out of it! You are too young to have a crush. He introduces himself as Jacob, asks me what I'm doing all alone, and once I tell him what I'm doing, asks if he can help. He says I can mount Twilight, the nightmare, and ride towards the mountains. When we reach the cave that the elixir is hidden in, we creep slowly into the first cavern, which is full of skeletons, but the ground slowly starts to shake. Jacob and I fall to the ground and by the time we look up, the entrance is covered by three-ton rocks. When we turn around, we see that we are surrounded by... wait for it... wait for it... BUNNIES!! !

Jacob starts to laugh, but he stops as soon as the bunnies' eyes glow red.

"Uh, Jacob," I ask, "Do you have a plan?"

He shakes his head no.

Leave it to boys to not be able to think during a crisis. It's always up to the girls to save the day.

"Run," I yell. "Do you not have any sense?"

Apparently he didn't. Jacob just stood there, not moving at all. I grab his hand and drag him across the cavern floor, but he still doesn't move his body at all. I am soooo falling out of like.

"Come on, Jacob," I plead. "Stop being a useless lump!"

Oh. My. Gosh. Boys are so annoying. Why did I fall in like with Jacob anyway?

"Jacob," I say, "Are you going to move, or do I have to wait until those evil, mentally-disturbed, red-eyed bunnies stampede?"

Apparently we were going to do the latter. The bunnies stampede, but soon they were stopped by the blinding-ness of my happy glow.

The room is pitch black.

When the cave finally lights back up, there stands Athena, shrouded in golden light.

"Medusa, you have shown tremendous courage here," she says. "I am proud to present you with the magic elixir."

Athena holds out a small vial with one drop of golden liquid, but just before she hands it to me, Jacob snatches it.

"My name is not Jacob," he says. "It's Perseus, the future hero of all of Greece, and my first act of good will be to destroy you!"

He lifts the vial up above his head and drops it. Falling, plummeting, descending, *CRASH!* The vial breaks and glass flies everywhere, but all I care about was the one drop of golden elixir disappearing into a crack. I start to weep and bow my head and the last thing I see is a glint of silver. Then everything goes black and I feel as if my form is disintegrating for one fleeting second before I feel nothing at all.

October 31st
Anana Walker, age 12

"Ok, class. Today, we will be talking about why Halloween was created as a holiday," said Mr. Smith.

"Woo-hoo," Jake said, sarcastically.

"That's right, Jake. Halloween was founded about 2,000 years ago by an angel by the name of Cassius. Now, Cassius defeated an evil demon named Samhain. Samhain was the meanest demon you could possibly think of. He possessed different people and things, such as pumpkins. People gave him candy to please him and wore masks to hide from him. If he found you, he would eat you and you would stay in his stomach for all of eternity." Just then, the bell rang. "Ok class, have a great Halloween. I'll see you next week," declared Mr. Smith.

"Hey Jake. What's up Lucas?" greeted Mark.

"Hey Mark," responded Lucas.

"So are we still on for Rachel's party?" asked Mark.

"Yeah. We'll meet up at Rachel's house before the party," said Jake, as he was about to depart. "See you guys later."

"Hello Batman," Rachel acknowledged Mark as he arrived at her house around 5:30 p.m., "And hello, Darth Vader," welcomed Rachel, to the masked person who was clearly Lucas. "And hello… farmer?" Rachel addressed Jake, who was wearing a green striped plaid shirt.

"You know what? Joke all you want to, but I think Halloween is lame. Now can we please just get started?" Jake sighed.

"Fine. Mark, you can get the decorations from the base—"

"Hey where's Cindy?" Lucas said, cutting Rachel off.

"Yeah. Where is she?" asked Mark.

"Oh, she texted me ten minutes before you came and said she's going to be late." Rachel replied.

"Of course she's late. It's Cindy. She's always late," said Jake.

"So, what if she's always late?" Rachel fired back at Jake.

"Guys cut it out, we need to get the party ready," Lucas exclaimed.

"Fine," Rachel said. "Mark, the decorations are in the basement. Lucas, I need you to pick up the sodas. Jake, I need you to hook up the sound system and I will get the food ready."

The friends were busy for a good thirty minutes getting everything together for the party, when an unexpected challenge appeared. "Ok, everything is rea-[the fuse box goes out]-dy, and Cindy is still not here," said Lucas.

"We should probably go check it out. Come on." Rachel ignored Lucas's comment. The group made their way to the fuse box only to find some of the wires unplugged.

"Jake did you unplug these?" questioned Rachel.

"Me? How could I? I was with you guys the whole time," assured Jake.

"You know what? It doesn't matter, just plug them back up," Lucas grumbled.

Everyone just sat there, waiting for someone else to fix the problem. After a few seconds of awkward silence, Lucas decided to act. But as he began plugging the wires back in place, something happened that made this particular October 31st one the group of friends would never forget. As soon as Lucas plugged in the last loose wire, a gargantuan spark shot out so big and bright that it blinded everyone in the room for a moment and knocked them down. When they slowly began to shake off the effects of the spark and get back on their feet, they looked around in shock and surprise! No longer were they in Rachel's house. They now found themselves in a strange neighborhood with people in costumes and others putting candy on their doorsteps.

"Where are we?" Jake uttered.

"Where are we? I think. *When* are we is the better question," stated Cindy.

"What do you mean by that?" responded Jake.

"I mean, look around you. There are no cars, no street lights, carriages being led by horses, and the people not in costumes are dressed like they are from ancient times, or some old fairy tale."

Everyone began to look around and realized she was right. They had gone back in time!

"Ah!" somebody screamed.

"Look over there!" Mark exclaimed.

"What's going on?" asked Rachel.

"I don't know, let's go check it out," Cindy told the group.

They walked towards the direction they heard the scream come from.

"Oh...my. ...gosh," they said in unison.

"What is that?" asked Jake

"That is Samhain," whispered Cindy.

"Sam-who?" asked Jake

"Samhain, the demon we were talking about in class," replied Lucas.

"Who dares speak my name?" Samhain questioned the group.

"I, Jake Foster, dare speak your name," Jake told him proudly.

"You, Jake, and your friends will face my wrath," spoke Samhain.

"I don't think so," said Lucas as he stood his ground.

Samhain used a malicious force to push them down.

"Ah," they all screamed as they fell back except Cindy. She didn't fall and she was glowing!

"Whoa. What's happening?" Mark asked.

"I don't know," replied Rachel.

Then Cindy drew some symbols and said some kind... of ritual and black smoke started coming out of Samhain's mouth until he fell down and collapsed.

"What just happened?" asked Jake.

"I don't know," Mark said, confused. "Oh, not again," he said and sighed, as they were blinded by the light again and were in school.

"Welcome back to class. How was your Halloween?"

Looking at each other, the group smiled slyly.

"Eventful, you could say," said Jake, who was now eager to learn the next lesson from his new favorite teacher.

"Okay, now we're going to learn about Thanksgiving..."

As the teacher's voice faded into the background, Lucas said, "Oh...

my ... gosh, Cindy was Cassius all along; the one that we were learning about. It all makes sense."

The Unintended Steal
Serena West, age 12

"Thank you for shopping at the Smithsonian Museum Store," said the cashier after she handed the cloth bag to Daniel.

Daniel Williams had just bought a replica of the Hope Diamond. The Hope Diamond is an absolutely gorgeous, deep blue diamond that hangs from a beautiful diamond necklace. In fact, the Hope Diamond is the largest known deep blue diamond in the world and worth over 200 million dollars! According to the legend, a curse occurred on "the King's Jewel" when it was stolen from an idol in India. The curse prophesied bad luck and death, not only for the owner of the diamond, but for anyone who touched it. However, none of this applied to Daniel Williams, because he only purchased a replica of the Hope Diamond.

Daniel Williams was on his plane back home to Manchester, England, when his flight started having terrible turbulences. During the turbulences, the replica of the Hope Diamond fell many times and Daniel wondered why the diamond never broke. Meanwhile in Washington, D.C., the Smithsonian was in an uproar because the transporters dropped the box that contained the genuine Hope Diamond. Since real diamonds don't break, they had nothing to worry about, right? To the museum's surprise, when they opened the box that held the precious jewel, part of the diamond was shattered like glass. They called all the world famous gemologist and jewelers to see if this could really happen, if this was even the true authentic Hope Diamond! The results were negative! The diamond wasn't real and it definitely wasn't the Hope Diamond. This is when the museum got the police involved and the search began. The police pulled up a list of all the people who went into the museum, thirty days before and right up to the actual day that it was discovered that there was a forged diamond in the case. The police went to the homes of all the people that recently visited the museum, except for one person, Daniel Williams. This is because the police couldn't find any information on Daniel, except for the fact that he purchased a replica of the Hope Diamond.

By this time now, Daniel Williams was at his house admiring his replica of the Hope Diamond. He turned on his television and these are the words Daniel heard on the news: "The Smithsonian Museum is temporarily closed because the Hope Diamond has been stolen and police authorities are looking for a possible suspect by the name of Daniel Williams." Even though Daniel knew he didn't steal the diamond, he feared police authorities were going to find out about other things in his life. Daniel didn't know what to do, so he just sat there holding the Hope Diamond and looking at the TV screen in awe!

Back at the Smithsonian Museum, the cashier that sold Daniel the replica of the Hope Diamond, was explaining to the police about how she sold a replica of the Hope Diamond to a man by the name of Daniel Williams, but she didn't know where the security camera footage (that would have been proof of her doing this) was located. The police searched for the security footage for a long time and eventually found it in a trashcan located at the back of the museum.

The police authorities took the long lost footage to a room in the museum and began to view it very carefully. After viewing the film closely, police authorities got a clear picture of Daniel's face. However, while the officers were looking at the tape, they saw something rather strange. They noticed that the cashier was slipping the Hope Diamond out of the pocket of her jacket and dropping it inside of Daniel's cloth bag. This raised a few eyebrows!

When the police interrogated the cashier about this, she admitted that she planned to take the bag home, but when she saw the security camera pointing right at her, she got scared and slipped the real Hope Diamond into Daniel's bag. She explained that out of fear, she took the tapes out of the camera and threw them into the trashcan. The officer continued to question her and asked, "But how did you plan on getting the Hope Diamond from this Daniel guy?" She started crying and said, "I don't know, I was so nervous and I really didn't have a plan. I guess I wasn't expecting anyone to purchase the replica. If he wouldn't have wanted to buy the replica, I think I would have gotten away with the true Hope Diamond!" The officer just shook his head and told the other officer to cuff her and take her downtown.

Through a lot of research and asking a lot of questions around town, the police authorities finally located Daniel Williams a couple of days later and paid him a visit. They interrogated Daniel to see who he really was because they didn't have any records of him in their files. It took a while, but Daniel finally told the officer that it was an alias—a false or assumed identity. Daniel's real name was George Broods. The police sentenced George to 35 years in prison, but George didn't make it 35 years. George couldn't handle the stress of being in prison, so he died of a massive heart attack two days later.

Once all the commotion was over, the museum framed the Hope Diamond and kept it heavily guarded. Now, even today, thousands of people's jaws drop and eyes glisten when they see the diamond that caused such an uproar and holds such a beauty! Still, many wonder, was it really stress that caused Daniel's (a.k.a. George) death or was it because he did, at one time, possess the beautiful, deep blue Hope Diamond!

Piece of a Masterpiece
Mackenzie Wilson, age 11

What's the Difference?

Mackenzie Wilson, age 11

We gain strength, courage, and confidence by each experience in which we really stop to look back, to think and compare. Middle school is a new experience that will make you think back, and that's when you realize the change. Elementary schools do have differences but many similarities too.

Middle school is much more complex, but there are so many things that will remind you of elementary, things that will never change. First, there are still those after school activities. Remember those sports you loved doing when school was over? Well, they're still here. However, there is still the same gross cafeteria food—still the accusations of mystery meat, moving food, and spots of green mold. Lastly, middle school still has classes for the over-thinkers or G.T. students. Although there may be more work in middle school, there are many similarities to elementary, but there are some major differences.

There is much more expected of you in middle school than elementary. In elementary, there are 1-2 different classes a day, while in middle school, because of the blocked schedule, there are 4 periods each day, every day. Also, there are about 2,000 kids in middle school whereas elementary has around 700 kids or less. Therefore, because of the massive difference in the numbers, there is about two teachers for a year in elementary while in middle school one person has eight teachers for a year. Since there are differences, this makes for a whole new experience that you may not remember from before.

As you can see, there are some things that will never change, but also things that will make the difference. In conclusion, no matter how hard you try, there will always be something just like the last and something to start a brand new adventure.

That Day
Courtney Young, age 11

That day full of love hate and heartbreak

Where we sat at the bridge the bridge of honey oak

Above the water looking down at the water like a

Mirror while we talked and talked about our

Future our hopes and dreams we sat there smiling

But that's before you told me which broke my heart

So I put on my shield so you wouldn't see just how

Much you meant to me but you're no fool so you knew

That I had put it on you told me to take it off so I did

But I wouldn't cry no way so we just sat there gazing

Into each other eyes while we sat there at the bridge

The Bridge of Honey Oak on that day

That Day

Worst Day Ever
Lauren Zamora, age 12

Beep! Beep! My alarm started blaring.

"Anna, it's time to wake up!" my mom screamed from the kitchen.

I couldn't remember why on earth I was waking up this early until my mom said I was going to be late for school. Once I heard that, I rushed out of bed like I had super speed and was on a sugar high. I had to take a bath, straighten my hair, and put a little makeup on. Most importantly, I had to pick out the perfect outfit to wear.

I glanced over at my pink and turquoise polka-dotted clock and saw I had only ten minutes to get ready or else I would be late for school. I decided to plug in the flat iron to let it heat up while I put on my makeup. The only problem was when I opened my makeup bag, all my makeup was mixed together. I could only put on my brand new bottle of mascara, which ended up giving me an allergic reaction so horrible, my eyes puffed up and I could hardly see. I still had to straighten my hair, but while I was doing it, I burned myself on my forehead, ear, and cheek. Now to top it all off, the outfit I was going to wear shrunk when my mom washed it yesterday. The top was dry clean only and the bottoms were not supposed to be dried. They needed to air dry. Instead of wearing the perfect outfit, I had to wear one of my least favorite outfits. I'm going to look like a freak when I get to school, a freak that has puffy eyes, a freak that has blisters all over their face, a freak that is wearing a non-fashionable outfit! What else could possibly go wrong? When the bus arrived at my house, I had mixed emotions. I felt excited and nervous. I was excited to meet all the new students and teachers. I'm also excited to meet up with all my old friends again. I was nervous because what would students think of me when they saw me on the bus or in the halls. They would think I was a huge freak because of my appearance. As I walked on the bus, everybody stared at me and then started whispering to each other. As I went to the back of the bus, I finally saw a friendly face—my best friend, Grace.

"What happened to your eyes? How did you get those blisters? Why on earth are you wearing *that* on your first day of school?" Grace said curiously.

"Well, first, my makeup mixed and I only had some mascara, which gave me an allergic reaction that puffed up my eyes so I could hardly see. Then, when I was trying to straighten my hair, I couldn't see, which made me burn myself. Finally, my mom washed the outfit I was going to wear today, but they shrunk. My top is dry clean only and my bottoms were not supposed to be dried, they needed to be air-dried."

About five minutes later, the bus arrived at school and my heart was pounding. What will everybody think of me when I got off the bus? Just as I suspected, some of the students were staring at me, and some of them were whispering to each other and pointing in my direction. As I was walking into the school, I wasn't paying attention and missed a step. I fell face first into the cement while my backpack went flying off and everything in it flew out. I was so embarrassed that I felt as red as a tomato.

As I was picking up all my materials, I noticed that I had ripped my pants and you could see my bright pink underwear. The first bell finally rang to go to first period so I was acting as if I knew where everything was, not trying to show that I was a hopeless sixth grader, completely lost. The tardy bell already rang and I was still wandering around. About ten minutes after the tardy bell, I finally found the right classroom. Or so I thought. I was in the classroom for about fifteen minutes when I finally realized that I was in the seventh grade science class. The teacher told a student to direct me to the sixth grade science room. When I got to the classroom, they had already learned one subject and when the teacher gave a quiz on it, I was the only one in the class that didn't make one-hundred percent.

The bell rang to go to second period so I rushed down the halls to find my locker. When I found my locker, I tried to open it about one-hundred times before I had to ask for help. When I got to gym class, I didn't know which was the girl's and which was the boy's locker room so, by accident, I went into the boys. Once again, I felt as red as a tomato as I was walking out of the boy's locker room.

After the horrible incident in gym class, I thought things would start to die down because I had lunch next. Maybe I just needed to eat something and then I would be less clumsy. I decided to get food from the lunch line and when it was my turn to pay, the lunch lady said, "no charge." This might start being a better day after all. I spoke *way* too soon. Not even a second later, I spilled my juice and it looked like I wet myself.

After lunch, I went to math class and was the only one in the class to make a one-hundred on the math quiz.

That's the moment things started going good for the rest of the day!

Prince Frazien

Oliver Nixon

Jonathan Rojas

Sandy Ramirez

Viviana Jorez

Vanessa Quezada

Ellis Havercamp

Marin Hart

Mackaye Wilson

Han Truong

michael Helfpauir

Jesus Pulido

Ella Berth

Sabrina Ramirez

Luis Fata

Natalie Prak

Sydney Bertrand

Isabel Pitts

Giggle Parker

Robert Ellis III

Jackson Guite

Laura... Phelps

Madeline Vanlandingham

Ellie Consolvo

Amara Walker

Louise Cohen

Keierra Hunter

Riley Avis

ADORA Goodheek

Serianna Hixson

Alina Coulter

Shelly Edison

Elyse Evans

Daniel Nunes

Madison Montgomery

Carolyn Ngo

Lauren Zamora

Edwin Panameri

ilda Rivera

Katherine Rodriguez

Braden Schey

Myles Brown

L. Burgher x

Damian Drabek

Jori Jones

Katherine Butler

Maya Poroni

Leslie Morales

Trinity Mosier

Joseph Dbisi

Haley Rodriguez

Shania Benjamin

Jaime Clara

Nadir Richardson

Serena West

Alizey Garcia

Agustin Mejia